Combat in the Stratosphere

Combat in the Stratosphere

Extreme Altitude Aircraft in Action During WW2

Steven Taylor

AIR WORLD

First published in Great Britain in 2024 by
Pen & Sword Military
An imprint of
Pen & Sword Books Ltd
Yorkshire - Philadelphia

ISBN 978 1 39903 693 1

Typeset in INDIA by IMPEC eSolutions
Printed and bound in England by CPI Group (UK) Ltd, Croydon, CR0 4YY

Pen & Sword Books Ltd. incorporates the Imprints of Pen & Sword Archaeology,
Atlas, Aviation, Battleground, Discovery, Family History, History, Maritime,
Military, Naval, Politics, Railways, Select, Transport, True Crime, Fiction,
Frontline Books, Leo Cooper, Praetorian Press, Seaforth Publishing,
Wharncliffe, White Owl and After the Battle.

For a complete list of Pen & Sword titles please contact

PEN & SWORD BOOKS LIMITED
47 Church Street, Barnsley, South Yorkshire S70 2AS, United Kingdom
E-mail: enquiries@pen-and-sword.co.uk
Website: www.pen-and-sword.co.uk

or

PEN AND SWORD BOOKS
1950 Lawrence Rd, Havertown, PA 19083, USA
E-mail: uspen-and-sword@casematepublishers.com
Website: www.penandswordbooks.com

MIX
Paper | Supporting
responsible forestry
FSC
www.fsc.org
FSC® C013604

Contents

Acknowledgements

For their permission to quote from various books, magazines, newspapers and websites, I would like to thank the following individuals, organisations and publishers: Nick Beale (whose website ghostbombers.com is an excellent source of information on the operational history of the Bf 109H); David Lauterborn at *Military History* magazine; Edd Moore at Reach PLC; Steve Manning of The People's Mosquito Ltd; Grub Street Publishing (*Luftwaffe Eagle*); Bloomsbury Publishing PLC (*Spitfire: Flying Legend* © Osprey Publishing); The History Press (*Focke-Wulf Fw 190 in Combat*; *One Of The Few*; *Spitfire: Pilots' Stories*); and Orion Publishing Group Ltd (*Wings On My Sleeve*).

For permission to reproduce images and illustrations, I'd like to thank: Jim Mitchell, Charlotte Junkers, Chris Goss, and BAE Systems.

Finally, I wish to thank the team at Pen & Sword Books.

Steven Taylor, October 2023
www.steventayloronline.co.uk

Glossary

A & AEE	Aircraft & Armament Experimental Establishment
ADGB	Air Defence of Great Britain
AFC	Air Force Cross
AI	Airborne Interception
Air Cdre	Air Commodore
AOC	Air Officer Commanding
ASI	Air Speed Indicator
Aufkl.Gr	Reconnaissance Group
AVM	Air Vice Marshal
C-in-C	Commander-in-Chief
CAS	Chief of the Air staff
Chutai	Squadron (Japanese)
CIOS	Combined Intelligence Objectives Sub-committee
CRD	Controller of Research and Development
DAF	Desert Air Force
DFC	Distinguished Flying Cross
DFM	Distinguished Flying Medal
DVL	*Deutsche Versuchsanstalt für Luftfahrt* (German Institute for Aviation Research)
E/A	Enemy Aircraft

Feldwebel	Sergeant
Flieger Hauptingenieur	Chief Flight Engineer
Fliegerkorps	Air Corps
Flight Lieutenant	Flight Lieutenant
Flying Officer/F/O	Flying Officer
Flight Sergeant	Flight Sergeant
GAF	German Air Force
GCI	Ground Control Interception
Gp Capt	Group Captain
Gruppe	Luftwaffe unit generally comprising about 30 aircraft
IAS	Indicated Air Speed
IJA	Imperial Japanese Army
IJN	Imperial Japanese Navy
JAAF	Japanese Army Air Force
Jabo	Fighter-bomber
Jagdgeschwader	Fighter Wing
JNAF	Japanese Navy Air Force
Kommando	Detachment
Leutnant	Lieutenant
MAP	Ministry of Aircraft Production
NF	Night Fighter
Oberfeldwebel	Flight Sergeant
Oberleutnant	First Lieutenant
Oberst	Colonel
Oberstleutnant	Lieutenant Colonel
OKW	*Oberkommando der Wehrmacht* (High Command of the German Armed Forces)

ORB	Operations Record Book
Plt Off	Pilot Officer
PR	Photo Reconnaissance
PRU	Photo Reconnaissance Unit
PVO	Soviet Air Defence Forces
RAE	Royal Aircraft Establishment
RLM	*Reichs Luftfahrt Ministerium* (German Air Ministry)
R/T	Radio/Telephone
Schräge Musik	Oblique-firing cannon
Sentai	A Japanese air group comprising 4–8 squadrons
Sqn Ldr	Squadron Leader
Staffel	Luftwaffe squadron of approximately 12 – 16 aircraft
Unteroffizier	Corporal
USAAC	United States Army Air Corps
USAAF	United States Army Air Force
VfH	*Versuchsstelle für Höhenflüge* (Experimental Centre for High Altitude Flight)
VVS	Soviet Air Force
Wg Cdr	Wing Commander
Wilde Sau	Codename for Luftwaffe tactic of using single-engine fighters lacking radar to intercept RAF bombers by night
W/O	Warrant Officer

Introduction

In 1902 French meteorologist Léon Teisserenc de Bort and German scientist Richard Assmann were jointly credited with discovering the stratosphere. In the northern hemisphere, the stratosphere is broadly defined as being the region of the atmosphere that begins at a height of around 33,000ft above sea level and extends to some 163,000ft above the Earth's surface, where it meets the mesosphere.[1]

Today, flying in the lower stratosphere is routine, both in military and civil aviation. But this was not the case in the Second World War. Due to the thin air at such altitudes (being many times less dense than that at sea level), flying in the stratosphere presented an enormous challenge, both in technical terms for the aircraft and in physiological terms for their crews. In the pre-war years much research had been carried out around the world into flight at stratospheric altitudes, while daring aviators from Britain, the United States, the Soviet Union, France, Italy and Germany competed with each other to set new world altitude records.

By the mid-1930s, advances in cockpit pressurisation and aircraft design, along with specially designed pressure suits, allowed pilots to reach what were then incredible heights of 40,000ft plus, the absolute world altitude record for a pilot flying a piston-engine aircraft being set at 56,000ft (by the Italian airman Mario Pezzi in October 1938). Helium-filled balloons carrying pressurised gondolas could reach even further into the stratosphere, Captains Albert Stevens and Orvil Anderson of the US Army Air Corps setting a world record of 72,395ft in their balloon *Explorer II* on 11 November 1935.

This race to achieve ever greater altitude was not undertaken simply for the purposes of national prestige and the personal glory of the aviators themselves, however. With rapid advances in the performance of interceptor fighters during the 1930s, it steadily became clear that speed alone would not be enough for the bomber or reconnaissance aircraft to survive in the airspace over the modern battlefield.

With war clouds once again gathering over Europe, a war in which air power was sure to play a central and, it was confidently predicted by some military theorists, decisive role, the major military powers grasped the obvious strategic benefits of having warplanes that could operate above the ceiling of the machines possessed by their potential enemies.[2] Equipped with the latest long-range, high-resolution cameras, reconnaissance aircraft could fly over hostile territory, taking their photographs without fear of being brought down by AA guns or defending interceptors, while waves of pressurised bombers cruising at 40,000ft and above could level towns and cities with impunity.

At the outbreak of the Second World War the leader in the field of pressurised military aircraft was undoubtedly Nazi Germany. Junkers' Ju 86P reconnaissance aircraft, developed from a lacklustre medium bomber of the mid-1930s, was the world's first combat aircraft equipped with a pressurised cabin to enter frontline service. For over two years, between August

1940 and September 1942, the Ju 86P and the later, improved R model were persistent thorns in the side of the Allies. Operating at heights of 39,000ft and above over the British Isles, the Soviet Union, the Mediterranean and North Africa, it proved to be virtually untouchable, giving the Luftwaffe a crucial advantage.

The introduction of the Ju 86P, and knowledge that the Germans were working on more advanced aircraft capable of reaching even greater heights, spurred Allied development of a host of specialised fighters designed with the sole purpose of intercepting this revolutionary spy plane. The British, in particular, invested heavily in such aircraft. Besides versions of two of the RAF's most legendary warplanes being optimised for high-altitude operations, the Supermarine Spitfire and de Havilland Mosquito, a dedicated fighter specially developed for shooting down enemy intruders at stratospheric altitudes, the Westland Welkin, was also put into limited production, after a protracted and troubled gestation.

Eventually, and with great difficulty, Allied pilots in North Africa managed to reach the operating height of the Ju 86R and shoot several down, achieving the highest altitude 'kills' of the Second World War. The Luftwaffe, however, were not discouraged and put considerable effort and resources into building a successor to the Ju 86P and R, one that could fly even higher.

In August 1942, meanwhile, long-held fears in Britain of enemy bombing raids from 40,000ft plus had become a reality, with the Luftwaffe adapting several of its Ju 86Rs to carry a modest bombload to conduct 'nuisance' raids (known as *störangriff*) over southern England and Wales by a special unit based in Beauvais in France, as a reprisal for Bomber Command's increasingly heavy and destructive raids on Germany.

The British and Americans also worked on a variety of high-altitude bomber projects of their own. As well as pressurised versions of Bomber Command's most successful aircraft, the Vickers Wellington and Avro Lancaster, the British also developed the Vickers Windsor, a heavy bomber intended from the outset to deliver its bombload from very high altitude. But it was the Americans who would produce the outstanding pressurised heavy bomber of the war with the Boeing B-29 Superfortress.

The belief in Nazi circles, encouraged by Allied propaganda, that this formidable bomber would be deployed to the European theatre served as the driving force behind the development of Germany's own series of high-altitude interceptors, or *höhenjägers*, which included the Blohm & Voss BV 155, the Focke-Wulf Ta 152H and the Messerschmitt Bf 109H model. Of course, when the B-29 did finally enter service, it would be used against the cities of Japan rather than those of Germany, forcing the JAAF and JNAF to try and come up with its own solution to the problem of defending its national territory from punishing enemy raids at high-altitude, including by the use of specially lightened fighters to ram the American bombers.

As defeat loomed for Nazi Germany, Hitler turned to his so-called 'vengeance' weapons in a last desperate bid to turn the tide of the war. But besides the V1 missile and V2 rocket, the Nazi dictator had another revenge weapon in mind with which to strike back against the British: a fleet of high-altitude bombers fitted with pressure cabins, which could circumvent the RAF's defences by relying solely on their great altitude. Heinkel, Henschel, Dornier and Junkers all responded to Hitler's call for high-altitude bombers, but like so many ground-breaking aircraft projects under development by the Germans in the latter stages of the war, time ran out for the Third Reich before the designs and prototypes they came up with could reach production.

Combat in the Stratosphere examines in depth the race between the Allied and Axis powers during the Second World War to produce both offensive and defensive warplanes that pushed back the boundaries of the maximum altitude attainable by propeller-driven aircraft – the jet aircraft of the war lie outside the scope of this book – and the air battles that took place in the stratosphere. It is also a tribute to the brave airmen on both sides who took these largely overlooked but revolutionary machines higher and higher into the dark blue skies, and in the process changed aviation forever.

Chapter One

The Quest for Altitude

In the pioneering early days of aviation, making and breaking altitude records became as much of an obsession for pilots as setting speed and distance records. The French aviator Roland Garros became a national hero when, in his Bleriot monoplane, he established a world altitude record of 12,960ft on 4 September 1911. A year later he smashed his own record, taking his Bleriot up to 18,410ft. Gallic dominance was not to last, however. Across the Channel the British were preparing their own assault on the title. Flying a specially modified Royal Aircraft Factory RE.5 reconnaissance aircraft with extended wings, South African-born Norman Channing Spratt of the Royal Flying Corps reached 18,900ft on 5 May 1914.

With the outbreak of war shortly afterwards, for the British the quest for altitude became a pressing necessity rather than simply a matter of national prestige, when the Imperial German Navy and Army launched a strategic bombing campaign against Britain using Zeppelin and Schutte-Lanz airships. Cruising at altitudes of up to 20,000ft, the Zeppelins often flew too high for the fighters with which the home defence squadrons of the Royal Flying Corps and Royal Naval Air Service were equipped, like the B.E.2c and B.E.12, to make a successful interception. Eventually, and with great difficulty, from September 1916 onwards home defence pilots managed to claw their way up to the Zepps' operating altitude to shoot down the giant, lumbering raiders.[1]

Besides the Zeppelins, in the latter part of the war Allied fighter pilots also had to contend with another groundbreaking German high-flyer. The Rumpler C.VII was designed as a long-range, high-altitude reconnaissance aircraft, which first appeared over the Western Front in late 1917. With a high-compression Maybach Mb IV engine, it had a maximum ceiling of 23,000ft, which it took around an hour to reach. Even more troublesome for the Allies was a variant known as the 'Rubild', a lightened C.VII which could reach an altitude of 24,000ft, putting it beyond the reach of Allied fighters. One Rumpler pilot, Otto Roosen, commented many years later: 'It was safe, high up there … most of the time.' The Rumpler crews were provided with electrically heated gloves and boots to cope with the cold in an open cockpit biplane (which could reach −30° Celsius), and rudimentary oxygen apparatus, consisting of a flask from which they would suck in oxygen through a tube, as Roosen explained:

> We had the oxygen tube feed into a face mask … You needed the mask to protect your face from the cold. Frostbite happened all the time with the Rumpler. Very dangerous. The mask, what is now called an oxygen mask, covered all our face from the goggles, extended around the chin and stopped at the neck. You would breathe from your nose or mouth. We may have been the first to have that.[2]

The C.VII's immunity was only seriously threatened when the British introduced the Sopwith Dolphin late in the war, which could – just – match the German aircraft's operating altitude.

The British equivalent of the Rumpler C.VII was the Airco DH.4, designed by the legendary Geoffrey de Havilland, which also entered service in 1917. The DH.4 served mainly as a bomber and reconnaissance type, a role for which its maximum ceiling of 23,000ft made it particularly well-suited. Like his German counterpart in the Rumpler, the DH.4 pilot performing high-level reconnaissance was equipped with electrically heated clothing, a leather facemask to prevent frostbite, and basic oxygen apparatus, which was used on flights above 16,000ft.

Record breakers

The coming of peace saw a resumption of record-breaking altitude flights with renewed vigour, as American, European and Soviet airmen competed with each other in a race to set the world altitude record. Often their records stood for mere months before being shattered again by their rivals. These daring aviators pushed themselves to the extreme limits of physical endurance in their efforts to climb ever higher towards the stratosphere.

In the 1920s the Americans were dominant. Towards the end of the First World War, the US Army Air Service set up the Engineering Division, which conducted experiments in high-altitude flight from McCook Field in Dayton, Ohio. Their star pilot was the 6ft 2inch tall Major Rudolph 'Shorty' Schroeder, the chief test pilot with the Division's Flight Test Section. He secured his first world altitude record on 18 September 1918, when he reached 28,900ft in a Bristol Fighter. Four more world altitude records were set by Schroder over the next eighteen months, the last on 27 February 1920, when he attained a height of 33,114ft in a Packard-LePere LUSAC 11 fitted with a turbo-supercharger and relying on similar oxygen apparatus as used by the German Rumpler crews. Upon raising his frost-coated goggles to change oxygen flasks, the moisture coating his eyeballs instantly froze in the −63° Celsius temperature, temporarily blinding him. Despite this, Schroeder succeeded in landing back safely at McCook Field.

Schroeder held the altitude record for nineteen months before it was broken by his countryman and fellow test pilot in the Engineering Division's Flight Test Section, Lieutenant John A. Macready. Flying the same LUSAC 11 aircraft, he climbed 1,300ft higher on 28 September 1921. This feat earned Macready the first of three prestigious MacKay Trophies, awarded to airmen for outstanding achievements in aviation. The test pilots of the Engineering Division would go on to set several more records over the next few years, including the highest altitude achieved by an aircraft carrying two people, when an experimental XCO-5 biplane reached 37,854ft on 10 October 1928.

These early record-breaking flights highlighted the extreme physical stress placed upon the pilot by flight at high-altitude. In the rarefied atmosphere above 30,000ft the pilot has to contend not only with extreme cold but also conditions such as hypoxia. This causes blackout and eventual loss of consciousness due to oxygen starvation; Schroeder was almost killed during his February 1920 flight when he passed out through lack of oxygen after his supply ran out. He regained consciousness and managed to pull his aircraft out of the steep dive it had entered with mere seconds to spare. Similarly, Macready complained of a 'slowing up' of his senses once he had climbed beyond 30,000ft and that his vision became 'dim and shaky', only returning to normal after descending to lower altitudes.

It had become clear that if greater altitudes were to be attained, and flight at stratospheric heights sustained for any length of time, the physiological problems associated with extreme altitude flying would have to be overcome.

As far as oxygen starvation was concerned, there were three solutions: the oxygen mask; the pressure suit; and the semi- or fully pressurised cockpit.

The oxygen mask provided no more than a partial solution. It became less effective at heights above 25,000ft, and the pilot would still have to endure the extreme cold at high altitude. The pressure suit seemed more promising. Scottish physiologist John Scott Haldane – who had invented one of the first gas masks used by the British Army in the First World War – first conceived of such a suit in 1920 and a working example was fashioned from a rubber diver's suit by the Siebe Gorman company, which specialised in deep-sea diving apparatus.

But the early pressure suits had a number of disadvantages, which Wing Commander Gerald Marshall, an RAF doctor specialising in physiology, outlined in a speech he gave to the Royal Aeronautical Society in 1933:

It would no doubt be mechanically possible, instead of seating the pilot in a sealed cockpit at relatively high pressure, to enclose his whole body in an impermeable suit, or his head and neck in a sort of diver's helmet. The helmet has the virtue of not requiring a special type of cockpit, but it has many disadvantages. It would be most unwieldy, it would inevitably interfere with the pilot's free movement to an undesirable degree, it would increase the respiratory problem of dead space, it would subject the pilot to different pressures inside and outside his thorax, so that resistance to inspiration would be reduced, and to expiration increased, and it would be very difficult to devise a fastening for it about the chest and shoulders which would be both airtight and readily detachable without excessive weight.[3]

Despite these drawbacks, in the mid-1930s the pressure suit concept was taken up with gusto by American aviator Wiley Post, who had gained fame as the first pilot to fly solo around the world. In 1934, Post enlisted the support of the rubber manufacturer B.F. Goodrich to develop one of the first practical full pressure suits for pilots, asking the company to design 'something like a diver's outfit, which the pilot can wear, and which can be blown up with air or oxygen to the required pressure'.[4]

The first two suits produced by the company's designers failed, one rupturing due to the air pressure, the other being too tight, with Post having to be cut out of it. The third suit was more successful, although it was found that when filled with air Post's mobility was severely restricted. Nevertheless, in a test flight on 5 September 1934 he demonstrated the capability of his experimental pressure suit when he reached 40,000ft in his Lockheed Vega (called 'Winnie Mae') while wearing one. Two months later he apparently breached the 50,000ft barrier, though the record could not be confirmed by the instruments in his aircraft.[5]

But as far as high-altitude aviation was concerned, the 1930s undoubtedly belonged to the Europeans, and the decade became something of a golden age for record-breaking. Cyril Uwins, chief test pilot at the Bristol Aeroplane Company, set a record of 43,976ft on 16 September 1932 in a modified Vickers Vespa VII biplane, earning him the Britannia Trophy. The following year the British achieved another historic first when Lord Clydesdale and David McIntyre flew over the world's highest peak, Mount Everest, in their Westland PV-3. Uwins record, meanwhile, was broken by Frenchman Gustave Lemoine on 28 September 1933, who attained 44,808ft in a Potez 506, before passing to Italy on 11 April 1934 when the Regia Aeronautica's Renato Donati achieved 47,352ft in a Caproni 113, fitted with a four-bladed propeller and a Bristol Pegasus engine.

These records were all set using modified versions of existing aircraft. But in 1936 Britain produced an aircraft specially developed for experimental flying at extreme altitudes. Designed by Frank Barnwell, who also designed the Blenheim bomber, the Bristol Type 138A was a low-wing monoplane, constructed mostly of wood and powered by a supercharged Pegasus engine. Wearing a full pressure suit equipped with a closed-circuit rebreather, RAF Squadron Leader F.R.D. Swain took off from the Royal Aircraft Establishment's airfield at Farnborough on 28 September 1936. 'I climbed in a series of wide circles and, looking down from about 46,000ft, I saw London like a little toy town, the Thames and other rivers like narrow ribbons, and the Channel Isles like small stones in a shallow riverbed. At that moment I felt very small and lonely,' he revealed in an interview conducted after the flight. Squadron Leader Swain eventually reached a height of 49,944ft, a new world record. But during the descent he encountered serious problems, as he explained:

> After descending about 5,000ft the celestroid window of my helmet and also the cockpit windows became covered with haze, and I was unable to see anything. This worried me, because I was unable to read the compass. I continued to descend rather erratically, and then I began to feel that I was suffocating and weakening. I pressed the release lever, which should have opened the cockpit cover, but it would not function. I could not lay my hand on the emergency zip fastener with which my suit is fitted, and I realised that there was only one thing to do. I got a knife, ripped the celestroid window of my helmet, tore away the rest of the celestroid, and breathed fresh air. My height was then 14,000ft, and as I only had two gallons of petrol, I landed.[6]

Eight more altitude records would be set with the Type 138A, the highest being 53,937ft, achieved by Flight Lieutenant M.J. Adam on 30 June 1937. Again, the flight very nearly ended in disaster when the pressure on the airframe at such an altitude caused the cockpit canopy to crack.

Flight Lieutenant Adam's record stood for sixteen months before being broken by Italian Mario Pezzi of the Regia Aeronautica, whose height of 56,046ft, set in a Caproni 161bis biplane on 22 October 1938, would remain the greatest altitude ever achieved by a piston-engine aircraft until the 1990s.

However, even equipped with a full pressure suit, such flights still imposed severe physical demands on the pilot. Besides hypoxia, at altitudes above 35,000ft, where the density of the air is extremely low, pilots can also become susceptible to decompression sickness – commonly known as 'the bends' – in which life-threatening gas bubbles form in the bloodstream. Common symptoms include fatigue, visual disturbances and joint pain, and in severe cases can lead to paralysis and death. Soviet pilot Vladimir Kokkinaki, who is believed to have reached 47,806ft in a Polikarpov TsKB-3 (a specialised variant of the I-15 biplane) in November 1935, is said to have claimed afterwards: 'Though my oxygen apparatus worked perfectly, it is not enough for the stratosphere. A single breath makes one realise this. Every movement requires great effort.'[7]

The answer was to equip aircraft with a pressurised cabin or cockpit. Cockpit pressurisation made sustained flight at altitudes in excess of 40,000ft possible, without the pilot succumbing to the debilitating effects of 'the bends', hypoxia, or other conditions associated with high-altitude flight. Pressurisation is a means of maintaining a safe level of oxygen for the crew by pumping a continuous flow of conditioned air into an airtight cockpit or cabin. For the crew, this creates the effect of flying at an altitude thousands of feet lower than the aircraft's actual height.

The first aircraft fitted with a semi-pressurised cockpit was the American USD-9A. A modified version of the British Airco DH.9A, it featured an airtight chamber for the pilot, into which oxygen was forced through small external turbines. Technical problems stymied Lieutenant John Macready's first attempt to carry out a flight in the aircraft, leaving Lieutenant Harold Harris of the Engineering Division to become the first pilot to fly the USD-9A, on 8 July 1921, from McCook Field. However, it would be some years before the technology was perfected and experimental aircraft with fully pressurised cockpits able to operate at heights in excess of 40,000ft took to the air. Among the early examples of such ground-breaking aircraft were Germany's Junkers Ju 49, the French Farman F.1001 and the Soviet Union's Chizhevski BOK-1, which first flew in 1936 and boasted a service ceiling of 46,260ft.[8]

These experimental aircraft could sometimes prove deadly to their pilots. On 5 August 1935, Frenchman Marcel Cagnot was killed while making an attempt on the world altitude record when his Farman F.1001 suffered a catastrophic decompression.

In the 1930s, technical advances in the field of aircraft pressurisation were to be of great benefit to the rapidly expanding commercial aviation sector. For the airlines, the advantages of pressurisation were that, at higher altitudes, aircraft efficiency is much greater, with less fuel being used in the thin air and consequently increasing the range. Airliners could also fly direct routes over mountainous terrain and avoid the worst of the weather and turbulence at lower level, increasing passenger comfort.

The first passenger aircraft with a pressurised cabin was the Lockheed XC-35. Converted from the company's successful

Electra Model 10 airliner, it was produced in response to a request from the US War Department issued in June 1936 for a 'Supercharged Cabin Transport Airplane', capable of maintaining flight at 25,000ft for a minimum of two hours. During test flights carried out in 1937 at the USAAC's test ground at Wright Field, Ohio, the single XC-35 produced met all the altitude requirements and earned the engineering team the Collier Trophy, awarded each year for the greatest achievement in aeronautics. The XC-35 went on to serve as the official air transport of US Assistant Secretary of War, Louis Johnson.

The first airliner with pressurisation intended for commercial service was Belgium's tri-motor Renard R.35, designed by Alfred Renard and pitched to the state airline SABENA to serve its routes to the Belgian Congo. Unfortunately, the only example of the R.35 crashed during a flight trial at Everes airfield near Brussels on 1 April 1938, killing the pilot, Georges Van Damme. The R.35 project died with him. More successful was Boeing's Model 307 Stratoliner, which made its maiden flight a few months later, on 31 December 1938. Using many parts from the company's B-17 'Flying Fortress' bomber, the Stratoliner became the world's first airliner with a pressurised cockpit and cabin to enter commercial service.

Work on pressurised civil aircraft was also ongoing in the United Kingdom, with General Aircraft Limited – best known for its light utility aircraft and military gliders – leading the way. To test the concept for a proposed airliner, the company built a pressure cabin into one of its twin-engine Monospar ST-25 Universal utility aircraft, with an auxiliary engine equipped with a supercharger driving the air compressor. On 11 May 1939 the GAL 41 became the first British aircraft with pressurisation to take to the air.

But as tensions between the European powers mounted during the late 1930s, minds were increasingly turning to the military potential of high-altitude aircraft, whose ceiling would put them beyond the maximum range of anti-aircraft guns and interceptors. For military purposes, however, aircraft with pressurised cabins had a number of disadvantages. They added weight to the airframe, thus degrading performance, were expensive to produce, and sudden decompression caused by enemy fire hitting the airtight cabin or chamber posed a serious risk to the crew, as Dr Herbert Wagner, a senior aeronautical engineer with the Junkers *Flugzeugwerke*, observed in his October 1937 report 'Construction of High Altitude Aircraft':

> The pressure in the chamber can be maintained even with slight leaks caused during the flight or by enemy fire; but if the leakage exceeds a certain limit, for example, if there is a hole 10cm in diameter or more, the compressors of the high-altitude engines are insufficient to maintain the pressure in the chamber. Injuries to the occupants, such as bursting of eardrums, etc., cannot be avoided and the aeroplane must descend to an altitude where standard oxygen equipment is sufficient.

Still, the advantages appeared to outweigh these problems. At a time when the bomber threat was dominating the thinking of the world's military strategists, the Germans were particularly attracted by the possibilities of fleets of bombers, equipped with pressurised cabins, attacking enemies from heights at which they would be virtually invulnerable. In his report, Dr Wagner also wrote:

> In these great altitudes, at various weather conditions it will be difficult to locate the aeroplane during approach flight by direct sighting or sound detectors. Thus it will be easier for a bomber approaching at high altitude to reach the target undiscovered and attack from a lower altitude. After the bombs are released, the aeroplane is light and its climbing speed will enable it in many cases to reach a high altitude for the return flight before being exposed to enemy fire ... As the flying altitude increases, the slight superiority of the light combat aeroplane [the fighter interceptor] over the bomber will become even smaller. The danger of fighter attacks on bombers is especially great on the return trip. However, on the return trip the bomber is light and its great wing area is an advantage over the fighter aeroplane as far as high-altitude flying is concerned.[9]

The Soviets were also attracted to the military potential offered by high-altitude flying, although in the years before the Second World War their interest lay primarily in the pressure suit. Yevgeny Chertovsky, an engineer at Leningrad's Aviation Medicine Institute who designed the Soviet Union's first pressure suit in the early 1930s, asserted: 'The protection [pressure] suits permit the creation of a stratospheric air force within a very short time. It will constitute a very potent war weapon, since all present ground defences are powerless against it.'[10]

Besides bombing, reconnaissance was another task for which aircraft capable of operating at very high altitudes held an obvious advantage. As a new generation of fast, heavily armed monoplane fighters entered service in the late 1930s, such as Germany's Messerschmitt Bf 109 and Britain's Hawker Hurricane and Supermarine Spitfire, it became clear that standard reconnaissance aircraft would have a very hard time operating over hostile territory defended by such fighters. This was driven home to the Luftwaffe during the 'Phoney War' period of 1939–40, when their standard reconnaissance types – mainly adapted bombers like the Dornier Do 17 and Heinkel He 111 – proved highly vulnerable to RAF fighters.[11]

Some reasoned that if the reconnaissance aircraft could not fly faster than the defending interceptor, it would have to fly higher, just as the Rumpler 'Rubild' had done during the First World War. Such high-altitude aircraft could also photograph their targets without the enemy even knowing they had been there. 'Aviation reconnaissance by an aggressor armed with the latest equipment can secretly reconnoitre the territories of a future adversary from great altitudes – even in peacetime,' argued Soviet military physician Vladislav Spasskiy in the mid-1930s.[12]

By the time the Second World War broke out, Nazi Germany had taken a decisive lead over its European rivals in the field of high-altitude military aviation, with the Luftwaffe becoming the first air force in the world to put into operational service a practical pressurised aircraft that could carry out reconnaissance at altitudes exceeding 40,000ft. In doing so, they would usher in a new era in military aviation and present a major challenge to the air forces tasked with protecting their nation's airspace against these stratospheric intruders.

Chapter Two

The Junkers Ju 86P

Although a pacifist and anti-Nazi, the aircraft company founded by German aeronautical engineer Professor Hugo Junkers would become synonymous with Hitler's war machine. Its Ju 87 Stuka dive-bomber spearheaded the Nazis' *blitzkrieg* invasions of 1939–41; the Ju 88 was the Luftwaffe's most versatile combat aircraft, serving as a bomber, heavy fighter, radar-equipped night-fighter, torpedo bomber and reconnaissance aircraft; while the trimotor Ju 52 formed the backbone of the Germans' transport fleet. In the interwar years Junkers also became a world leader in the field of high-altitude research.

The Junkers *Flugzeug und Motorwerke* AG (Junkers Aircraft and Engine works), established in the city of Dessau in eastern Germany, made its mark during the First World War, when it gained a reputation for innovative designs and aeronautical concepts. Rejecting the wood and fabric construction of all other military aircraft of the period, in 1915 Junkers produced the world's first practical all-metal aeroplane, the J 1 (nicknamed the 'Tin Donkey'). Having proven the concept, Junkers went on to produce the first all-metal combat aircraft, the almost identically named J.I, which entered service in 1917. Boasting a robustness that would become a hallmark of the company's products, the J.I featured an armoured 'bathtub' type cockpit for the crew, made of 5mm thick high-grade steel, with further armour-plating around the vital areas, making it capable of absorbing considerable battle damage and so proving particularly effective in the ground-attack role. British engineers from the Air Ministry who examined captured examples after the war were impressed by the machine. 'It is evidently a serious attempt to reduce to a minimum the dangers due to enemy action while in flight, and to lengthen the life and endurance of the machine in spite of exposure to bad weather and to rough handling,' their report stated.[1]

Prohibited from possessing an air force under the terms of the Treaty of Versailles, after the war German aircraft manufacturers like Junkers diversified into the growing civil aviation sector. One of their most successful designs in the interwar period was the W 34 commercial transport, which was introduced in 1926 and went on to set a world record for flight endurance in August 1927. A modified variant of this aircraft, fitted with a Bristol Jupiter VII radial engine, was used for high-altitude flight research. On 26 May 1929, Junkers test pilot and First World War ace Wilhelm 'Willy' Neuenhofen set a world altitude record of 41,795ft in the W 34, with the aid of Dräger oxygen apparatus.[2]

Impressed by Junkers' achievement, the DVL provided the funds for the company to develop an experimental aircraft specifically for research into flight at very high altitude. The aircraft the Junkers team came up with was the Ju 49. Powered by an L88a V-12 engine with a two-stage supercharger and intercooler, the Ju 49 featured a removable pressure cabin, which accommodated a two-man crew. One problem with this cabin was the crew's very limited visibility through its five small porthole windows, leading to the addition of a periscope to aid the pilot's view. Construction of the sole example (which carried the civil registration D2688) was completed in the summer of 1931, becoming only the second aircraft in the world to be fitted with a pressure cabin. On 2 October of that year the Ju 49 made its first test flight. In November 1933 it reached 32,808ft, one of the engine cylinders cracking during the flight, and in 1937 attained a height of 41,010ft. Ultimately, however, the Junkers team considered the aircraft only a qualified success. 'While the Ju 49 did not reach the expected especially high altitudes,' wrote Dr Wagner, 'it nevertheless furnished numerous experiences as to pressure chamber and high–altitude engine.'[3]

The Junkers team was primarily concerned with the application of cabin pressurisation for the benefit of commercial aviation, where Professor Junkers' main interest lay. However, when the Nazis came to power and embarked on a colossal rearmament programme, at the heart of which was building up a new air force, the Junkers company inevitably became drawn once again into military aviation. Considered politically unreliable, Professor Junkers was placed under house arrest in 1934 and passed away the following year, aged 76, by which time the Nazis had taken full control of his company.

Over the next few years the Junkers company developed the aircraft that would go on to become the backbone of Hermann Goering's Luftwaffe in the Second World War. And its pioneering work in the field of pressurisation meant that the firm was ideally placed when Germany's Air Ministry, the

RLM, became interested in developing aircraft for extreme altitude operations.

The EF 61

Junkers' first attempt at building a warplane with a pressurised cabin was the *Entwicklungs Flugzeug* ('Development Aircraft') 61, or EF 61, work on which began in 1935. Intended as a high-altitude reconnaissance aircraft and *schnellbomber*, the requirements set out for the EF 61 by the RLM were that it should have a maximum speed of 311 mph, a service ceiling of 39,370ft and be capable of carrying 2,200lbs of bombs over a range of 1,200 miles.

Powered by two Daimler-Benz 600A V-12 engines, the airframe was constructed mostly of corrugated metal, like the company's famous Ju 52. One of the biggest challenges facing the Junkers team during construction of the prototype was to build a pressure cabin with sufficient visibility for the crew to be able to bomb targets accurately. 'Therefore,' explained Dr Wagner, 'we designed a pressure chamber whose entire front part was to consist of a plastic dome.'[4] Incorporating any glass was ruled out 'since panes of such size and shape could not be manufactured and would splinter.' Ordinary Plexiglas, on the other hand, would not withstand the pressure at high altitudes. A solution was provided by I.G. Farben, which developed a new, especially tough plastic called 'Reilit'.[5] To overcome one of the perennial problems of extremely high-altitude flight – condensation or icing forming on the windows – warm air from the engine was pumped into the space between the two layers of glazing.

The first of the two EF 61 prototypes that were built made its maiden flight in March 1937. But on a high-speed test flight on 19 September 1937 the aircraft was written off after the crew encountered controllability problems at an altitude of 11,400ft, caused by buckling of one of the ailerons, and were forced to bale out. Three months later the second prototype also crashed on a test flight. With the demise of this second prototype, the EF 61 project was abandoned.

But the Luftwaffe's enthusiasm for high-altitude aircraft had not diminished, and the search for another aircraft to fulfil the role continued.

A Failed Bomber

Rather than design an all-new aircraft from scratch, it was decided to adapt an existing airframe for high-altitude work. With their extensive experience in the field, inevitably Junkers would step up to fulfil the Luftwaffe's need. The platform their engineers chose for the basis of this new high-altitude aircraft was the Junkers Ju 86.

The Ju 86 emerged from a Luftwaffe requirement for a medium bomber capable of carrying 2,200lbs of bombs, issued in early 1934. Junkers submitted a proposal based on a civil airliner it was already working on, and the company was awarded a contract to build five prototypes. Designated the Ju 86 and designed by a team under Ernst Zindel, head of the Junkers design bureau, the first prototype was ready within six months and made its maiden flight from Dessau on 4 November 1934. In July the following year it was sent to the Luftwaffe's test centre at Rechlin for thorough evaluation.

What Zindel and his team produced was a conventional, twin-engine 1930s bomber, whose most unusual features were a retractable ventral gun turret (nicknamed 'the dustbin') and its powerplants. Unlike most military aircraft, these were diesel engines – Jumo 205s (though the first prototype was fitted with Siemens SAM 22 motors, due to delays in the delivery of the Jumos). Diesel engines had the advantage of being considerably more fuel efficient than petrol ones. But the Jumo 205s proved temperamental, having a tendency to overheat during hard manoeuvring.

Although judged an inferior machine to Heinkel's rival He 111, with the Luftwaffe's expansion proceeding apace the Ju 86 was ordered into production. Several variants were produced, from A to G models (the Ju 86E replacing the Jumo 205 diesels with BMW 132 engines, while the Ju 86G introduced a glazed nose to improve pilot visibility). Around 850 rolled off the Dessau assembly line before production ceased in 1938.

The Ju 86's baptism of fire came in the Spanish Civil War. Five examples joined the Luftwaffe's Condor Legion from February 1937, which had been sent to Spain to assist General Franco's Nationalist forces against the Republican Government. Initially based at Seville, they served alongside He 111s and Do 17s in *Versuchsbomberstaffel 88*, or VB/88, an experimental bomber squadron set up to test Germany's new twin-engine bombers under operational conditions. It was to be an inauspicious combat debut for the Junkers machine, however. Reliability issues with the Jumo diesel engines dogged the Ju 86's time in Spain and, after suffering several losses, they were withdrawn a few months later. The surviving examples were passed on to Franco's Nationalist Air Force.

By the outbreak of the Second World War only one frontline *Gruppe* was still equipped with the type. They were taken out of service in the bomber role at the end of the Polish campaign, the Luftwaffe choosing to focus on the more dependable He 111 and Junkers' new *schnellbomber*, the Ju 88, as its standard medium bomber types. Many of the remaining Ju 86s were used as instructional airframes for training bomber crews, while fifty-eight equipped two transport *Gruppen* hastily formed to help resupply the besieged Sixth Army during the Stalingrad airlift in the winter of 1942/43, in which they suffered heavy losses. A few others were used for anti-partisan duties in Yugoslavia.

The Ju 86 was also widely exported, the military export version being assigned the designation Ju 86K. A total of sixty-six were ordered by the Royal Hungarian Air Force, taking part in the brief Slovak-Hungarian War of March 1939 and on the Eastern Front once Hungary had joined the German-led invasion of the Soviet Union. The Ju 86 was also one of the few aircraft of the Second World War to see action on both the Axis and Allied side. The South African Air Force requisitioned seventeen Ju 86Z airliners operated by South Africa Airways in 1939. Converted into bombers with the addition of external bomb racks and Vickers .303 machine guns, they were assigned to No 12 and 16 Squadrons, serving alongside a single Ju 86K bought by the SAAF for evaluation purposes in 1938. No 12 Squadron's Ju 86s flew their first operational mission, against

Italian forces in Abyssinia, on 16 June 1940. The SAAF retired its surviving Ju 86s in 1942.

A stratospheric spy plane

With the Ju 86 proving a disappointment in its original function as a medium bomber, Junkers looked for another role for their unloved diesel aircraft, and in September 1939 submitted a proposal to the RLM to convert a small number of the airframes into high-altitude reconnaissance aircraft, with a projected ceiling of 40,000ft. Recognising the obvious benefits of such a machine, the RLM gave its blessing and awarded Junkers a contract to produce forty examples of the high-altitude variant, based on the 'G' model, which was given the designation Ju 86P. It was produced in two versions: the P-1, which was configured for bombing, and the P-2 reconnaissance aircraft.

The nose section was rebuilt to incorporate a pressurised cabin designed to accommodate the two-man crew – a pilot and a navigator/wireless operator – the engines were replaced with two Jumo 207 A-1 six-cylinder inline diesel motors, each producing 950 hp, and the gun positions were all deleted. The first prototype, known as Ju 86 PV-1 (serial number D-AHUB), made its initial test flight in February 1940 with Junkers test pilots Kurt Heintz and Ernst Seibert, during which it reached a height of 32,800ft. However, Junkers' engineers realised that a greater altitude could be attained with an increased wingspan. And so the third prototype, PV-3, had its span extended from the standard 74 to 84ft. This version reached 39,700ft in test flights, taking fifty-four minutes to reach its maximum altitude.

It had a top speed of 248 mph, an endurance of six-and-a-half hours and a maximum range of 1,100 miles.

Extensive testing of the Ju 86P prototypes was conducted at Rechlin and at the *Versuschsstelle für Höhenflüge*. Established in 1939 at Oranienburg, twenty miles north of Berlin, the VfH was a Luftwaffe facility for carrying out research into high-altitude aviation, including all aspects of pressurisation and baling out of aircraft at extreme altitude. It also evaluated captured enemy aircraft. By the beginning of August 1940 a total of forty-three flights at heights above 33,000ft had been carried out with the Ju 86P prototypes.

Over the course of the next two years the Ju 86P series underwent several modifications in an effort to eke out more altitude from the aircraft. In 1941 work began on the improved R-1 model. Among the changes this version introduced were upgraded Jumo 207 B-3 diesel engines, four-bladed VDM propellers in place of the earlier three-bladed ones, and a wingspan that was lengthened still further, to 105ft. These modifications allowed the aircraft to reach 45,900ft. The first example of the Ju 86R-1 variant was delivered in November 1941.[6]

The Ju 86P was not, however, universally popular with its crews. The noise and smell of the diesel engines was a common complaint, as was the fragility of the airframe. 'The wings were of enormous span and tended to flex considerably,' explained Leutnant Erich Sommer, who served as a Ju 86 navigator in 1942. 'Because they were liable to fold under very little stress, we were told to go easy when manoeuvring.'[7] Neither was the famous British test pilot Captain Eric 'Winkle' Brown overly impressed when he flew a captured example after the war.

'It was not a very impressive aeroplane to fly, frankly, apart from the fact that it had the pressurisation and the engines to get you up to higher altitude,' he commented. 'And it was a laborious aeroplane to get up to any height at all. I would say lumbering would be the right word to describe how it felt on the controls … It was obviously built on the assumption that it would not be attacked.'[8]

Despite its shortcomings from a pilot's point of view, with the Luftwaffe's standard reconnaissance aircraft, the Heinkel He 111H and Dornier Do 17P and F (*Fernerkunder* – long-range) model, proving highly vulnerable to interception by British and French fighters during the 'Phoney War' period and the subsequent Battle of France, the Ju 86P was seen by Luftwaffe commanders as the solution to stem their steady losses.

Chapter Three

Kommando **Rowehl**

In 1938, the Commander-in-Chief of the German Army, General Werner Freiherr von Fritsch, stated that 'the military organisation that has the best photographic intelligence will win the next war.'[1] When war came just a year later, the air force with the best photographic intelligence was undoubtedly the Luftwaffe. And that was due almost entirely to the efforts of one man: Theodor Rowehl.

Born in Gottingen in 1894, Rowehl served as an observer in the air arm of the Imperial German Navy during the First World War. In 1930, now a civilian aviator, he was hired by the German intelligence service, the Abwehr, to form a clandestine aerial reconnaissance unit to secretly photograph military and industrial targets throughout Europe, using civil aircraft operating under the cover of the aerial mapping company Hansa Luftbild. One of the aircraft he used to carry out recce flights along the Polish border was the specially modified Junkers W 34 Willy Neuenhofen had used to set a world altitude record in 1929.

Impressed by his work, in 1935 Hermann Goering personally invited Rowehl to join his newly unveiled Luftwaffe, with the rank of Hauptmann. His unit was given the title Special Purposes Squadron, and came under the command of the Luftwaffe's 5th Branch (Intelligence). The role of the unit remained the same, however: covert photographic reconnaissance of strategic targets, using aircraft bearing civil markings, including the newly introduced Heinkel He 111s of the state airline *Deutsche Lufthansa*.

As political tensions across Europe grew, so did the size and scope of Rowehl's outfit. Soon the unit was operating three *staffeln*, of 12 aircraft each, its area of operations extending from the United Kingdom to the Soviet Union. With the outbreak of war in September 1939 and the need to disguise its existence having largely disappeared, the unit came out of the shadows a little. Given the official designation *AufklärungsGruppe des Oberbefehlshabers der Luftwaffe* (Reconnaissance Group of the Luftwaffe High Command), shortened to Aufkl.Gr.ObdL, it was more informally known as the *Kommando* Rowehl, and by that time contained a mix of He 111s, Do 17s, Ju 88s, Fw 200 Condors and Do 215s (an improved version of the Do 17). Among the targets photographed by Rowehl and his hand-picked group of pilots were defensive fortifications along the French-German frontier. The work of the *Kommando* Rowehl was judged to be a major factor in the success of Nazi Germany's *blitzkrieg* campaigns in Poland, Scandinavia, the Low Countries and France.[2]

One of the more ambitious missions undertaken by the *Kommando* Rowehl in the first months of the war was a PR sortie from Bulgaria to Syria in early 1940, after Goering received intelligence reports warning that an Anglo-French bomber force was assembling in the Middle East to strike at the Russian oilfields in the Caucasus, which at the time was providing much of the Luftwaffe's oil. The reconnaissance flights had been personally ordered by Goering, as he later revealed when questioned on the subject at the Nuremberg war crimes trial:

> I had received more and more news that there were to be undertakings ... against the Russian oilfields of the Caucasus and Baku. I received these messages about the intentions of these Franco-English aircraft squadrons to be sent there [to Syria] ... and thus to strike the Russian oilfields most severely and eliminate them.

Rowehl's pilots were able to confirm that the British and French were indeed gathering a large force of bombers on airfields in northern Syria, and Goering testified at Nuremberg that with this photographic proof he was able to warn Hitler 'so that Germany would draw Russia's attention to the danger it was facing'.[3]

In recognition of his achievements Rowehl was awarded the Knight's Cross in September 1940, by which time he had been promoted to Oberst.

The Battle of Britain

In the summer of 1940, however, the Luftwaffe faced its sternest test to date as it clashed with the RAF in the Battle of Britain. Carrying out reconnaissance in the fiercely contested skies over southern England was proving difficult. On 30 August, a Do 215 of the *Kommando* Rowehl was shot down near Norfolk by

Spitfires of No 66 Squadron. A day later another of the unit's Do 215's was lost, again falling to the guns of a 66 Squadron Spitfire. So the addition of the new Ju 86P-2 to the *Kommando* Rowehl's inventory in August 1940 couldn't have been more timely.

Equipped with three Zeiss Reihenbildner Rb 50/30 and Rb 75/30 cameras, mounted in the rear section of the fuselage, two Ju 86Ps were listed among the aircraft operational with the *Kommando* Rowehl on 13 August 1940 ('Eagle Day'), stationed at Orly, just south of Paris.

The Ju 86P's operational debut proved to be an unqualified success. Over the next two months they photographed airfields, ports and industrial targets in southern England and the Midlands, without loss. Among the *Kommando* Rowehl pilots who flew the Ju 86P over England in 1940 was Siegfried Knemeyer. One of the most successful German reconnaissance pilots of the war, Knemeyer had flown some of the earliest PR missions to the British Isles after the commencement of hostilities, earning the Iron Cross for a daring sortie to the Orkneys to photograph the Royal Navy base at Scapa Flow in October 1939.

The RAF was at first unaware of the high-altitude spy flights being carried out over Britain; in 1940, the Chain Home radar network that monitored the nation's airspace was incapable of detecting contacts flying at the Ju 86P's altitude.[4] But by 1941 it was realised that the enemy were conducting reconnaissance over the country using an aircraft capable of flying at unusually high altitudes. The problem confronting Fighter Command was how to reach and shoot down this high-flying spy plane. The most advanced interceptor then equipping Fighter Command's squadrons, the Spitfire Mk II, had a maximum ceiling of 37,000ft, comfortably below the Ju 86P's operating altitude. Nor could even the most powerful guns of Anti-Aircraft Command threaten the high-flyer. 'With our present equipment, we are unable to engage enemy targets much above 30,000ft,' lamented General Frederick Pile, C-in-C of Anti-Aircraft Command.[5]

At the time, British intelligence on these stratospheric intruders was sparse. 'The state of our knowledge on these [high-altitude aircraft] is far from satisfactory,' the RAF's Air Intelligence Branch frankly admitted.

> It would be of great value if any combat reports on encounters with aircraft at unusual altitudes could be notified to this section. In particular, any observations or pilot's estimates of speeds and rates of climb of these aircraft in comparison with our own may give a useful guide to their performance and may possibly help in predicting further developments.

Over the next few months Air Intelligence gradually gleaned more information on the Ju 86P, based on aerial reconnaissance of enemy air bases, interrogation of captured Luftwaffe aircrew who knew about the aircraft, and signal intercepts. A report compiled by the Air Intelligence Branch stated:

> It is known that specialised high altitude reconnaissance aircraft were being developed for the G.A.F. before the war ... A great part of Germany's experimental work

on high-flying aircraft for bombing and reconnaissance appears to have been assigned to the Junkers concern. Several years ago this company built a monoplane which broke the world's altitude record and since that time has taken out a number of patents on devices associated with sub-stratospheric flying.[6]

It soon became clear that the elusive reconnaissance aircraft was an adaptation of the Ju 86 bomber, of which the RAF was already very familiar thanks to its use by the South African Air Force.

Development work was based on the proven Ju 86 design. Originally built in two distinct forms (as a commercial transport and bomber) the Ju 86 was later supplied to South Africa as a convertible type which, although normally a transport machine, could be quickly adapted for bombing. Ju 86 bombers have been used with success by the S.A.A.F.

The report continued: 'A German source states that the Ju 86P is "a special development of the Ju 86 G-0, G-1 type." It differs from this, in essentials, in that the engine is a Jumo 207A; it has a sealed cabin, no armament is installed.'

Interrogation of a Luftwaffe PoW also revealed that 'a special emergency boost device is used to improve climb in the event of attacks by fighters. The figure given in this connection is an increase of altitude of 2,000ft in a very short period of time.' This referred to GM-1, a power boost system developed by the engineer Professor Otto Lutz of the German Aeronautical Research Institute and nicknamed Goering's *Mischung* (Goering's Mixture). By injecting liquified nitrous oxide into the supercharger, it increased an aircraft's performance at high altitude. One drawback of the system, however, was that it added additional weight and made the aircraft's handling more sluggish.

Then, later in 1941, the British received an intelligence windfall when they managed to acquire a copy of the official Ju 86P operator's manual, allowing Air Intelligence to build up a fairly detailed picture of the type.

> It appears that the basic structure is almost identical with that of earlier machines of the Ju 86 series … The engines fitted are of the Jumo 207 A/1 liquid-cooled diesel type … In principle, the Jumo 207 conforms with previous Jumo diesel practice, i.e. it is a 6-cylinder, opposed piston type with six common combustion chambers. A turbo-blower of large diameter and a scavenging blower appear to be installed to the rear of the engine and an object which is probably an induction air cooler is fitted to the induction system … It is thought that the maintenance of Ju 86 high-altitude aircraft is very complicated and, therefore, the serviceability figure comparatively low.

Naturally, the pressure cabin was of particular interest to the intelligence analysts:

> The pressure cabin appears to extend aft to a bulkhead of the leading edge of the wing. Pressure is automatically

regulated to about 0'72 atm [atmospheric] abs [absolute] corresponding to a height of 3000–3500 m, when this height is exceeded a red warning light illuminates and a warning horn is sounded. In the roof of the pilots' cabin, apparently extending to port and starboard sides, is an emergency exit which must be properly closed by hexagonal screws, for which there is a key on the switchboard. A sliding window is mentioned and must 'remain open'. The pilot and wireless operator are provided with special clothing suitable for high-altitude flying and for parachute descent from a great height ... both men wear parachutes equipped with oxygen apparatus. Before a parachute drop is undertaken the pressure could be equalised by pulling the appropriate lever and opening what is termed the 'summer ventilation valve'. If a parachute with oxygen equipment is available this should be set working before the jump. If there is no such provision it is advisable to carry a portable breathing apparatus in the small cabin for use in descent. If even this is not possible the aircraft oxygen apparatus should be used before the jump. The parachute should not be opened until a height of 4,000 metres has been reached.[7]

The report went on to point out that, according to the manual, 'aerobatics are prohibited' and that 'special emphasis is laid on the fact that "sharp pulling out and other excessive strain on these aircraft must, in all cases, be avoided." The aircraft must be handled in flight in the same way as normal commercial and transport aircraft.' The report also observed that 'the engines operate on diesel oil and the risk of fire from incendiary ammunition is considerably reduced.'

The report concluded rather dismissively that, 'Although the Ju 86P ... is undoubtedly interesting and worthy of close study, it can hardly be considered a brilliant technical achievement. It is likely that the type is considered as a "stop-gap".'[8]

However, its success during the Battle of Britain was indisputable. Although the number of missions flown by the Ju 86Ps of the *Kommando* Rowehl was quite small, none were lost in action – making it the only German aircraft type to emerge from the Battle unscathed.

Operation Barbarossa

The Soviet Union had been one of the principal targets for the *Kommando* Rowehl since the unit's formation. Hitler had ordered a suspension of Luftwaffe overflights of Soviet territory while the Battle of Britain was underway, but when it became clear that the Luftwaffe had failed to achieve air superiority over the island, forcing the cancellation of his planned invasion of Britain, he rescinded this order in October 1940, allowing penetrations of Soviet airspace up to a depth of 320 km. And with preparations for the Nazi invasion of the Soviet Union gathering pace, the Ju 86Ps of the *Kommando* Rowehl were to play an important part in reconnoitring key Soviet targets in advance of Operation Barbarossa.

Between October 1940 and June 1941 German reconnaissance aircraft regularly overflew Soviet territory. By spring 1941 the

Soviets were recording an average of three intrusions per day. At first, the German reconnaissance crews faced little danger as Stalin, wary of provoking Hitler, had ordered his air force to ignore the intruders. One Soviet fighter pilot who disregarded this decree and attempted to intercept a Ju 88 on a secret recce flight was said to have been arrested and court-martialled. But as the Luftwaffe stepped up its overflights, Stalin relaxed his ban on interceptions.

On 15 April 1941, pilot Leutnant Albert Schnetz and his navigator Leutnant Walther took off from their airfield in Cracow, Poland in a Ju 86P, carrying civil markings and the serial D-APEW, on a high-altitude sortie to photograph Zhytomyr in Ukraine. At 39,000ft, near Rovno in Soviet-occupied eastern Poland, they began experiencing engine trouble. Forced to descend, their Ju 86P came down to a height at which it could be intercepted by a pursuing MiG-3 fighter, which opened fire. Accounts differ as to whether or not the MiG actually hit the Junkers, but the result was that the spy plane was forced to make an emergency landing in a field. The crew had standing orders that, in such an event, they were to destroy the aircraft and camera equipment using explosive charges to conceal from the Soviets the true purpose of their flight. But Schnetz and Walther failed to complete this task before Russian soldiers arrived at the crash site and took them prisoner. When news of the Ju 86P's loss reached him, Goering flew into a rage.[9]

The two airmen were taken away for interrogation by the NKVD secret police. Sticking to their cover story that they belonged to a flight training school in Cracow, Schnetz and Walther insisted they had accidentally strayed into Soviet airspace while on a routine training flight. Still being held in a Soviet prison when the Germans launched Operation Barbarossa two months later, as German forces advanced they were told by their captors that they were to be executed. Amid the general chaos of the Soviet retreat, however, they were left behind by their guards. Joining up with friendly forces, the fortunate airmen soon returned to their base in Poland.[10]

The Ju 86Ps continued to fly reconnaissance missions over the Soviet Union, with little interference from the VVS. But in the spring of 1942 several of the high-flyers were transferred to another theatre of operations, where their immunity from interception was to be seriously challenged for the first time.

Chapter Four

Flying from Kastelli

I n the spring of 1941 the RAF began construction of an airfield near the village of Kastelli in Crete, fifteen miles southeast of the capital Heraklion, in anticipation of a German assault on the strategically important island in the eastern Mediterranean. After Crete was captured by the Germans in their successful – if costly – airborne invasion in May (Operation Mercury), the Luftwaffe picked up where the British had left off and completed work on the air base. Comprising three airstrips, it was home to Ju 88 torpedo-bombers and night-fighters, as well as Bf 109s, which carried out operations over the eastern Mediterranean.

In late May 1942, four of the improved Ju 86R-1s arrived at Kastelli, attached to 2.(F)/Aufkl.Gr.123, which also operated Ju 88Ds in the photo-recce role. Bolstering the Luftwaffe's PR capabilities in the region was vitally important at this time, with the war in North Africa entering its most critical phase as Field Marshal Erwin Rommel's Afrika Korps threatened to push the British and their allies back to the Suez Canal.

Having received no advance warning of the Ju 86Rs deployment to the Mediterranean from RAF Intelligence, the appearance of these mysterious intruders flying at altitudes of 40,000ft plus came as quite a surprise to the pilots of the Desert Air Force fighter squadrons stationed in Egypt. Many of the

DAF squadrons were equipped with the Hurricane IIB, armed with twelve .303 Browning machine guns and optimised for the ground-attack role. With a service ceiling of around 33,000ft, it posed little threat to the Ju 86R.

One of the first encounters with the Ju 86R in the Middle East was by the Hurricane IIB-equipped No 1 Sqn of the South African Air Force, stationed at RAF Idku in Egypt. On the morning of 4 June 1942, two Hurricanes were scrambled to intercept when radar picked up a contact flying close to their base at very high altitude, the pilots misidentifying the enemy aircraft as a Heinkel He 177, the Luftwaffe's notoriously problematic heavy bomber. The Squadron's Operations Record Book recorded:

> when they sighted him, they were at their ceiling, 33,000ft, and he was still about 7,000ft above them. The bandit was emitting a heavy white trail from each engine, and was plainly visible passing over the aerodrome. Capt. Metelerkamp [the squadron's second-in-command] went up but was also unable to reach him. By comparing notes afterwards the three pilots were certain that the bandit was a He 177.[1]

To improve their ceiling, the ground crews of No 1 Squadron set about lightening one of the Hurricanes by removing eight of the twelve Browning machine guns, as well as its armour plating, in the hope the German high-flyer 'may be reached and engaged instead of merely escorted by a pilot who looks up longingly at it'. Known as the squadron's 'lucky' Hurricane, the fighter reached 34,500ft during a practice flight before going into a spin, from which the pilot recovered at 23,000ft.

Over the next few days several attempts were made using this and other similarly lightened Hurricanes to intercept the Ju 86Rs – 'shufti-kites', as the DAF pilots dubbed them – which were making almost daily PR runs over the area. On 12 June, Pilot Officer Foskett was scrambled when an aircraft was tracked flying at very high altitude over Alexandria. The Squadron's ORB explained:

> As Foskett climbed, so the Bandit climbed, emitting a heavy white trail, and maintained a height of 8,000ft above the Hurricane, otherwise ignoring him. 'Jerry' circled Alex [Alexandria] deliberately and then flew towards Port Said. When Foskett reached 36,000 (indicated) he dived and climbed, making four such attacks from below, until he had exhausted his ammo. This is the fourth time that the He 177 [*sic*] has been seen. On this occasion too it was clearly visible from the aerodrome.[2]

Attempts were also made at this time to destroy the aircraft at Kastelli on the ground. On the night of 8 June 1942, an SBS raiding team under the command of Captain George Duncan was landed on Crete by motorboat to sabotage the aircraft and facilities at Kastelli. It was one element of a larger plan to attack all the major air bases on the island in coordinated commando raids. Although the raid on Kastelli was a success, with Captain Duncan's team destroying five aircraft, several transport vehicles, bomb stores and one large fuel dump, without suffering any casualties, it's thought that none of the aircraft put out of action were Ju 86Rs. Three days later an RAF raid on the airfield at Kastelli destroyed a single Ju 88.

The identity of the snoopers flying overhead at very high altitude remained a mystery, despite several of the squadron's pilots who attempted intercepts being able to provide fairly detailed and accurate descriptions of the Ju 86R. 'Much argument still goes on as to the type of recce e/a which comes over with impunity every day,' No 1 Squadron's ORB recorded. RAF Air Intelligence at Middle East Command in Cairo 'inclines to the view that it is a Ju 88. Our pilots are sure that it is not.'[3]

But, finally, the Air Intelligence Branch learned that the mystery aircraft was a Junkers Ju 86R-1.[4] Since the type's first appearance over England almost two years earlier, British Intelligence had learned quite a lot about the Ju 86P and R models, and a report was passed on to Middle East Command, which highlighted the aircraft's weaknesses to help the fighter pilots of the Desert Air Force deal with the new threat.

It is important to stress the vulnerability of the high-altitude Ju 86 and it seems unlikely that the air compressors are sufficient to counteract any appreciable damage to the cabin. There is no mention of armour protection on this aircraft. Even if an attempt were made to fit some form of protection it would probably be very light as otherwise the climb and ceiling would be affected. Therefore it would seem that as long as it could attain and maintain an altitude of about 42,000 to 43,000ft a fighter with a light armament should easily deal with the high-altitude Ju 86P.[5]

But after several more failed attempts at interception, it became clear that even stripped of armour and most of its armament, the Hurricane IIB was never going to attain enough altitude to bring down a Ju 86R. Wing Commander John 'Johnny' Kent, a Battle of Britain ace who commanded 17 Sector at RAF Benina in Benghazi in 1943, later wrote that, 'The Hurricanes with which the squadrons were equipped were virtually useless when it came to try to deal with the high-flying German machines and interceptions were continually being missed.'[6]

It was obvious that an aircraft with superior high-altitude performance would be required if the Desert Air Force was to bring the Ju 86R spy flights to an end.

Fortunately, Britain's most effective fighter was about to join the fray.

Enter the Spitfire

For the Allies, the situation in North Africa was becoming critical. On 21 June 1942, Tobruk fell to Rommel's Afrika Korps and the British Eighth Army was pushed back to defensive positions at El Alamein. In the air, although outnumbered, the Luftwaffe's Bf 109s were inflicting heavy losses on the Desert Air Force, while the Ju 86Rs on Kastelli were a persistent thorn in the Allies' side, their regular reconnaissance flights giving Rommel a priceless advantage.

There was, however, one bright spot in the otherwise gloomy picture. In March 1942 the first Spitfires arrived in Egypt, and on 16 June the DAF's 103 Maintenance Unit based at Aboukir, which serviced, repaired and tested the aircraft of the Desert Air Force, formed a High Altitude Flight, initially comprising three Spitfire Mk Vcs (serials BP985, BR114 and BR234), to help bring the Luftwaffe's high-altitude reconnaissance flights from Crete to a halt.

However, with a service ceiling of around 37,000ft, the Mk V still could not reach the Ju 86R's operating altitude. So, as with the Hurricanes, the Spitfires were lightened by stripping them of everything deemed non-essential. The two 20mm cannon in the wings were removed, reducing the armament to four .303 Browning machine guns; ammunition was reduced to 150 rounds per gun; armour plating was removed and the standard battery was replaced by a much smaller, lighter one taken from a field radio. Even after this lightening work had been done, the closest one of the Spitfires got was 2,000ft below the Ju 86R. When the pilot tried to raise the nose of his fighter to fire a burst, the Spitfire stalled.[7]

And so further modifications were carried out on the Mk Vs to increase their ceiling. The amount of ammunition carried was reduced still more, down to just fifty rounds per gun; the wingtips were extended at Aboukir by the engineers of 103 MU to give the aircraft extra lift; and by shaving a sixteenth of an inch off the cylinder head it was found that a little extra power could be extracted from the Rolls-Royce Merlin engine. These refinements helped one of the unit's test pilots reach 40,000ft and damage a Ju 86R on 27 June 1942. Although the German managed to regain his base at Kastelli, this was the DAF's first tangible success against the Ju 86R and proved that the Spitfire could reach the high-flyer, even if the pilot would have to endure temperatures of around −67° Celsius at that altitude.

The pilot of the intercepting Spitfire was Pilot Officer Eric 'Jumbo' Genders, who would become an important figure in the DAF's battle against the Ju 86R. Born in Oldham in 1920, Genders already had a distinguished combat career. Joining the RAF Volunteer Reserve in 1939, he served in the Hurricane-equipped No 33 Squadron in Greece in April 1941, where he was credited with destroying three Ju 87s and a probable Bf 109 during the German invasion of that country. He added two more 'kills', both Ju 88s, during the subsequent Battle of Crete, making him an 'ace'. In North Africa he increased his tally, downing a pair of Fiat G.50s of the Regia Aeronautica on 17 June and a Savoia–Marchetti SM.79 bomber five months later. These successes earned him a Distinguished Flying Medal in April 1942, shortly before he joined 103 MU as a test pilot. His citation read:

> This airman has taken part in operations over Greece, Crete and the Western Desert with great courage and determination. In the course of these operations he has destroyed at least 7 enemy aircraft and damaged several others. He has set an excellent example to junior pilots in the squadron.[8]

The size of 103 MU grew with the addition of several pilots from No 123 Squadron. It was one of these pilots who achieved

103 MU's first 'kill' on 26 July – although the victim was not a Ju 86R but a Ju 88A of 1(F).122, also based at Kastelli, which was shot down by Pilot Officer Alistair Wilson. A few days later the same pilot intercepted and fired on a Ju 86R, but on this occasion his target slipped away.

By August, with the Eighth Army's newly appointed commander General Montgomery building up his forces in Egypt in preparation for the decisive battle of El Alamein, it was imperative that the Axis forces be denied aerial reconnaissance, and so the DAF's effort against the Ju 86R was stepped up. In July, No 145 Squadron, also equipped with Spitfire Vs, joined the struggle against the Ju 86R. On 10 August one of its stripped Spitfires was scrambled, the pilot making visual contact with a Ju 86R at 36,000ft but was unable to intercept. Four days later another was sighted at 38,000ft, but 'too far off for interception'.[9] Another squadron operating specially lightened Spitfires was No 601, based at RAF Helwan, which attempted an intercept of a Ju 86R on 14 August. '1 Spitfire, specially modified for high altitude flying, took off to intercept an enemy aircraft (probably Ju 86 fitted with pressure cabin), followed aircraft for some time but was short of petrol and landed at Aboukir.'[10]

To further increase the Mk V's operating altitude, the amount of fuel carried was reduced. It was also decided to remove one of the last heavy pieces of equipment, the R/T set. This necessitated the development of a new tactic. Two fighters would be scrambled on each intercept – known as a 'marker' and 'striker' aircraft. The 'marker' (either a Spitfire or Hurricane), still equipped with R/T, would remain in contact with Ground Control and be vectored towards the Ju 86R, flying below the target to mark its position for the stripped Spitfire (the 'striker') to carry out an interception.

The new tactic was tried out on 20 August 1942. Around midday, a Ju 86R was tracked flying along the entire length of the Suez Canal at 200 mph, photographing shipping in the canal, before heading northwest to Alexandria. A 'marker' and a 'striker' Spitfire of 145 Squadron were scrambled. At 36,000ft the pilot of the 'marker' aircraft spotted the white smoke trails produced by the Junkers' diesel engines 6,000ft above him and helped guide the accompanying 'striker' Spitfire, flown by Sergeant Duigan, into an attacking position. Duigan climbed to 40,000ft and came within ten yards of the Ju 86R. But after firing just a single round his guns froze. Duigan then resorted to a desperate tactic in his determination to bring down the enemy aircraft, as the squadron record book explains: 'He tried to ram the tail of the Ju 86 but got caught in the slipstream and lost 1,000ft of height.' The fortunate Ju 86R crew escaped and the frustrated Duigan was forced to return to base.[11]

On 24 August the Spitfire pilots came tantalisingly close to finally bringing down their first Ju 86R, when one of 103 MU's test pilots, Flying Officer George Reynolds, gave chase to a Junkers flying north of Cairo at 37,000ft. The crew gained more altitude to try to shake off their pursuer but Reynolds matched the German's climb, despite the intense pain he was experiencing. At 42,000ft he opened fire and observed hits. The Ju 86R banked away, smoke pouring from one engine. At this point, Reynolds blacked out, regaining consciousness at around 32,000ft. With his oxygen supply and petrol almost exhausted, he returned to base, landing with just five gallons left in his tank. Although it was reported at the time (and in numerous accounts since) that the Ju 86R subsequently crashed in the desert, the pilot of the damaged aircraft, Hauptmann Bauer, managed to land safely on one engine.

Three days later Reynolds attempted to intercept another Ju 86R, possibly damaging it in the process, though again the enemy recce aircraft slipped away. Shortly afterwards, Reynolds was awarded a DFC, partly in recognition of his efforts against the Ju 86Rs, as the award citation stated: 'In addition to normal duties, this officer has completed numerous sorties in the Middle East against enemy reconnaissance aircraft flying at great altitudes … Flying Officer Reynolds has displayed a high standard of skill and devotion to duty.'[12]

As it became clear to the Germans that the Ju 86R could no longer rely solely on its great height for protection, defensive armament in the form of a single 7.92mm MG 17 machine gun was added, positioned in the rear fuselage and fired remotely from the cabin. However, this modification did little to lessen the danger. On 29 August, pilot Hauptmann Helmut Rammig and his observer Leutnant Günther Kolw were on the return leg of a PR sortie to the Suez Canal in their Ju 86R when they reported engine trouble. Losing altitude, they were forced to ditch in the Mediterranean about 100 km south of Crete, from where they were rescued by a Dornier Do 24 flying boat. A Spitfire V flown by Pilot Officer Genders was pursuing Rammig's aircraft as it left the Egyptian coast, firing a brief burst before his guns froze, but it remains unclear if the Ju 86R's loss was due to Genders' fire or mechanical problems.

No doubt surrounds Genders' dramatic destruction of another Ju 86R just a week later, however. At 1120 hrs he was scrambled from Aboukir to intercept one of the intruders in a 'striker' Spitfire, which lacked a radio and carried a reduced fuel load to achieve maximum altitude, while a fellow 103 MU pilot, Pilot Officer Arthur Gold, flew the 'marker' aircraft. They sighted the Ju 86R about fifty miles east of Alexandria, at an altitude of 40,000ft; 'the Germans must have seen us,' Genders revealed in his combat report, 'as they began to fly back again over the sea'. Genders gained height and began his attack with short bursts every three minutes from below. But after reaching 37,000ft, his port gun stopped and his engine lost power. Undeterred, after climbing again he made a second attack at close range. 'I concentrated on the right engine and saw bullets striking it,' he reported. 'When I had finished my ammunition and broke away, I noticed the Ju 86 was losing height and that there was a great deal more smoke from the st'bd [starboard] engine than the port engine.'

As the German descended, Pilot Officer Gold was able to inflict further damage to the Ju 86R. The crew made an emergency landing in the desert in an area held by German forces. The pilot and observer were uninjured but their aircraft was damaged beyond repair and was later destroyed by the retreating Germans when Montgomery's offensive at El Alamein drove them back. Pilot Officer Gold made a safe landing back at Aboukir with only a few gallons of fuel left, but Genders' troubles were only just beginning.

Running out of fuel while still well out over the sea, he glided for a few miles before baling out of his Spitfire at 1,000ft, landing in the water about ten miles from the Egyptian coast. Several rescue planes were launched to search for the missing pilot, one coming within a few hundred yards of his position, but although he 'splashed a great deal, they did not see me,' he later stated. Forced to swim all the way to shore, he finally reached land twenty-one hours later, where the exhausted airman was found by two locals who were out shooting birds. After a week's leave, he returned to his unit.[13]

Meanwhile, the battle against the Ju 86Rs continued. Three days after Genders and Gold's joint 'kill', Flying Officer Reynolds chased and attacked what he identified as a Ju 86 at a height of over 40,000ft. The physical toll flying at such extreme altitude took on the pilot was described in a subsequent DAF report: 'His body was wrenched with pain, his arms were temporarily paralyzed and his eyesight for the moment almost failed with weakness.' Despite this state of semi-paralysis, when he came within range of his quarry as it raced back towards Crete over the Mediterranean, Reynolds 'managed to move his hands sufficiently to press the firing button'.[14] Reynolds ran out of fuel shortly before reaching his base, but managed to glide the rest of the way and land safely. Although the report claimed the Ju 86R was destroyed, Luftwaffe records do not support this. Reynolds' victim may instead have been a Ju 88D from the same unit, which was lost that day while on a reconnaissance flight to Port Said.

On 15 September it was Pilot Officer Gold's turn again to have another crack at a Ju 86R, opening fire at 44,000ft when he closed to within range of the enemy intruder. Though he reported hitting the Junkers' port engine, it was not brought down.

To assist the fighter pilots of the Desert Air Force in their ongoing battle with the Ju 86R, a report was compiled from accounts of airmen who had successfully intercepted the high-flyers, highlighting both the strengths and weaknesses of the type, based on their combat experiences. Among other things, the report was able to confirm that the type was unarmoured. 'The crew of Ju 86s have been wounded, according to Intelligence Reports, by fire of aircraft carrying only two rifle-calibre M.G.s firing A.P. [Armour Piercing] and de Wilde ammunition.'

However, the report continued:

We do not think the Ju 86 is as fragile as has been suggested. The Ju 86 appears to be able to carry on, on one engine without losing much height. On September 6th he was attempting to reach his base on one engine when a Spitfire caught up with him 135 miles North of Alexandria at 37,000ft. He was heading due North at that time after another Spitfire had disabled his engine at 40,500ft. He seemed to be able to maintain his height and work pressure cabin on either engine. On September 6th it was his starboard engine that was stopped, and on September 15th his port, and on each occasion he was getting along nicely.[15]

The report also argued that the widely held belief that the Ju 86P and R models were unmanoeuvrable at high altitude was mistaken, pointing out that during the interception on 15 September the Ju 86R whose port engine had been put out of action by Pilot Officer Gold's Spitfire 'carried out violent evasive action including a dive from 39,000ft to 36,000ft quite steeply during which the A.S.I. was certainly more than 185 [mph] and probably about 240, and then climbed to 37,000ft in a climbing turn – on one engine.'

The report also addressed some of the problems associated with high altitude flying and offered advice on how to reach the Ju 86R's operating height.

> When the climb gets very slow towards the end the pilot is apt to get impatient and through coarse movements of the controls lose height which is so hard to gain and at the same time lose speed, so that he thinks he has reached the ceiling before, in reality, he has. After about 34,000ft there is no cloud and seldom any horizon so that it is difficult to hold the aircraft [at an] absolutely steady attitude, but when it comes to following the Ju 86 he can be used as an 'aiming mark' in lieu of cloud or horizon with the result that the aircraft can be held rigidly in its correct attitude and the aircraft then appears to climb up effortlessly until a time his altitude is reached.[16]

A Ju 86R was lightly damaged while making a landing at Caleto in Rhodes on 11 November and another was more seriously damaged on 14 February 1943 when engine failure forced pilot Oberleutnant Franz Hessinger to carry out an emergency belly-landing at Timbaki in southern Crete.

While the Axis position in North Africa rapidly deteriorated during the first few months of 1943, culminating in the capture of much of the Afrika Korps and the Italian army in Tunisia in

May, the Ju 86Rs were still going about their business relatively untroubled by Allied fighters. On 7 June 1943, for example, a pair of Spitfires of No 80 Squadron were scrambled in response to a Ju 86R flying over Alexandria at 45,000ft. 'White 1, Sergeant Stephen, reached 35,000ft and fired 50 rounds from his cannons when the hostile reduced his height to 42,000ft, but as Sergeant Stephen spun off immediately after firing and the hostile was 6,000 to 7,000ft above no strikes were observed.'[17]

No 123 Squadron, based at Bu Amud in Libya, was experiencing similar frustration. Their Spitfire Vcs attempted to intercept a Ju 86R on the afternoon of 19 June 1943, chasing it for '20 – 30 miles without getting within 900 yards of him. He just flew snootily along 2,000 [ft] above the Spits all the way. This was annoying.' After several more failed attempts to reach the Ju 86Rs over the next few days, the Squadron's Operations Record Book remarked in frustration: 'There doesn't seem to be a great deal of use sending them [Spitfires] up at all.'[18]

'Exasperating machines'

Wing Com Kent's own experiences of trying to counter the enemy high-flyers from his base in Libya during this period, which he recounted in his memoirs, reflected those of the Egyptian-based Spitfire pilots:

On one occasion, after a long chase, I managed to coax my Spitfire up to an indicated 41,500ft but was still about 1,000ft below and slightly behind a Ju 86P. While the Spit appeared to have reached its absolute ceiling, the German aircraft was still slowly climbing away so, in desperation, I pulled up the nose of my aircraft and fired a burst hoping that a lucky shot might bring down the enemy machine.

I do not know what became of the Junkers but, as I fired, my machine shuddered, stalled and flicked into a spin from which I was unable to recover until we had reached 20,000 ft. Although this sort of thing was repeated by various pilots without strikes being seen we must have been hitting these exasperating machines as at one time, according to an intelligence report, all the Ju 86Ps based on Crete were unserviceable with bullet-perforated cabins.[19]

Kent was correct. Although the pilots didn't know it at the time, combat damage and accidents were having a deleterious effect on the serviceability of the small force of Ju 86Rs, with seldom more than two being available at any one time for operations. And the Ju 86R crews' problems were about to get worse as several of the latest Spitfire Mk IX variant reached 103 MU that summer.

Essentially a Mk Vc fitted with the more powerful Merlin 61 engine with a two-stage supercharger to give it an improved ceiling, the Mk IX was only intended as an interim model to combat the Focke-Wulf Fw 190, which the RAF was struggling to deal with. But it proved so successful that it would become the second most produced Spitfire mark. An assessment by the RAF's Air Fighting Development Unit, dated April 1942, revealed that the Mk IX's high-altitude performance was particularly impressive:

> Several climbs were made to heights between 39,000 and 40,000ft and the pilot felt that the aircraft was capable of going even higher. Although the operational ceiling is considered to be 38,000ft, it is thought that Sections of two could operate up to 39,000ft and probably higher. The aircraft is easy to fly at high altitudes, but freezing up of the trimming tabs occurred. It was therefore difficult to keep the aircraft level as it was still trimmed for climb. During manoeuvres there is otherwise little tendency to lose height even at 38,000ft.

The report concluded that 'the performance of the Spitfire IX is outstandingly better than the Spitfire V, especially at heights above 20,000ft'.[20]

The verdict of the pilots who flew it in combat was equally complimentary. Johnnie Johnson, one of the RAF's highest-scoring aces of the Second World War, considered the Spitfire IX to be the best of all the Spitfire marks. That view was shared by another famous RAF ace with an illustrious wartime record, New Zealander Al Deere.[21]

Two Mk IXs of 103 MU, attached to No 80 Sqn at Gamil and flown by Australian Flying Officers Harry Freckelton and Hal Rowlands, were scrambled on 2 July 1943 along with a pair of 80 Sqn's Spitfire Vcs, flown by Flying Officer Hunter and Pilot Officer Pratley, to pursue a Ju 86R shadowing a convoy north of Alexandria. After being attacked at high altitude by the Mk IXs, the damaged aircraft was forced to descend, where the two Spitfire Vcs were waiting to finish him off, as the No 80 Sqn ORB explains:

> F/O Hunter made several attacks at 31,000ft and set the hostile aircraft on fire and obtained strikes on the fuselage. It finally disintegrated in the air, burning furiously, and fell into the sea. We claimed one half-destroyed. P/O Pratley also engaged the enemy and claimed to have assisted in its destruction. He had engine trouble and baled out and was picked up by a convoy escort ship and taken to Beirut, suffering from slight burns. He rejoined the Squadron 10 days later.[22]

The Ju 86R's crew, pilot Leutnant Franz Stock and his observer Unteroffizier Heinz-Udo Kannenberg, both perished.

Five days later the squadron had another encounter with a high-flyer. Four Spitfire Vcs and a single Mk IX were sent up after the enemy aircraft, flying at between 42,000 and 45,000ft over Benghazi. But there was to be no repeat of their earlier success. The Mk IX, piloted by Flying Officer Ken Watts, got closest, opening fire at an altitude of 40,000ft but 'the bandit still had a safe margin of height and escaped'. Feeling 'hazy and dozy' due to lack of oxygen, Watts landed back at base where, almost unconscious, he had to be lifted out of the cockpit by medics.[23]

It was a similar story on 19 July, when the Mk IX was again scrambled to intercept what was thought to be a Ju 86R, flying at 40,000ft plus. By the time the Spitfire reached the same altitude, the enemy aircraft was out of range and escaped.

Meanwhile, No 123 Squadron at Bu Amud, which had repeatedly failed to intercept the regular Ju 86R flights with its Mk Vcs, also received a Mk IX, much to the delight of the unit's personnel. 'Our prayers are answered,' the Squadron ORB recorded on 3 July, 'a real live Spit IX turns up complete with pilot from 451 Squadron.' However, on the squadron's next scramble in response to a Ju 86R flight the following day, annoyingly the Mk IX was grounded due to mechanical problems.[24]

On 29 July the recently appointed new CO of 103 MU, New Zealander Flight Lieutenant Jeff West DFM, went after another Ju 86R in a Mk IX, after it was spotted heading towards Derna at 45,000ft. Accompanying him were two No 80 Sqn pilots, Flight Sergeant McCloy and Sergeant King, flying Mk Vcs. After a thirty-minute chase, in which they were unable to get beyond 35,000ft, McCloy and King were forced to break off. In his Mk IX, however, West managed to get within 2,000ft of the enemy's height and opened fire, only for his port gun to freeze after a brief burst. A follow-up attack was similarly unproductive, a burst from West's sole functioning gun throwing his Spitfire out of balance and causing it to lose altitude, allowing the German to slip away.

Flight Lieutenant West enjoyed greater success when he next tangled with a Ju 86R, on 6 August. At a height of 41,900ft, while some 500ft below the Junkers, he opened fire, even though he had only limited forward vision through his iced-over cockpit canopy. As before, one of his cannon stopped after firing a few rounds. He made another attack with his remaining gun shortly after and this time 'observed a strike on the starboard tail unit', before that gun too froze and his damaged prey escaped north.[25]

This was one of the last encounters between the Spitfires and the Ju 86Rs over the Mediterranean. By September 2.(F)/123 was down to a single serviceable Ju 86R and few more, if any, reconnaissance flights were carried out in this theatre by the type. With the Allies having captured Sicily in July, precipitating the overthrow of Mussolini, and carrying out successful landings on the Italian mainland in September, the German position in the region became increasingly precarious. The Spitfire pilots' suspicions that they had been inflicting damage on the Ju 86R high-flyers was confirmed after the Allies liberated Greece in 1944 and captured two badly shot up Ju 86Rs on Tatoi airfield near Athens, where the remnants of 2.(F)/123 had moved to the previous year. While these were the first examples of the Ju 86P/R series to fall into Allied hands, RAF intelligence officers noted with disappointment after an inspection of the airframes that 'the pressure cabin was so badly damaged that very little information could be obtained'.[26]

Chapter Five

Strato Spits

Even before the Ju 86P had made its first appearance in British skies in August 1940, Air Chief Marshal Sir Hugh Dowding had been concerned about the threat posed by pressurised enemy aircraft which could operate at very high altitudes, beyond the ceiling of his Hurricanes and Spitfires. On 22 June 1940 he expressed his fears in a letter to the Air Ministry, writing that the Germans could soon put into service 'a new series of four-engine bombers which will have a ceiling in the neighbourhood of 35,000ft'.[1] He returned to the theme in a despatch he wrote in August 1941 for the Air Ministry about the Battle of Britain and the lessons learned for the future of the country's air defence. 'We must be prepared,' he warned, 'for the appearance of the pressure-cabin bomber, flying at a height unattainable by any non-pressurised fighter.' He added:

> Of course, a pressure-cabin bomber is inefficient and vulnerable, because it is difficult to operate free guns from a pressure cabin, and pressure leakage from holes made in the walls of the cabin will prostrate the crew. The threat from pressurised bombers is therefore serious only if we have no fighters to meet them, and for this reason we should always possess a limited number of pressurised fighters.[2]

To meet this expected challenge, at a meeting of Air Ministry officials in February 1941 it was decided that a specialised variant of the Spitfire with a pressurised cockpit should be produced exclusively for the high-altitude interception role. These 'Strato Spits', as the famous Free French fighter ace Pierre Clostermann would later dub them, should have the ability to reach 40,000ft.[3] At a later meeting the Ministry of Aircraft Production stated a requirement for 350 of these aircraft, 'with a trickle to follow to make up wastage. A very definite requirement is for two squadrons before the end of 1941.'[4] With the project being accorded a high priority by the Air Ministry, the Supermarine design team under their chief designer Joe Smith immediately got to work.

Known during its development as the Supermarine Type 350, Smith's team took a standard Spitfire Mk V, put in a more powerful Merlin 47 engine – which was capable of producing 1,415 hp – and replaced the three-bladed propeller with a four-bladed Rotol constant-speed one. The most radical alteration, however, was the incorporation of a pressurised cockpit with a Marshall compressor to blow air into the cockpit, which would allow the pilot to survive at heights above 35,000ft. Unlike the other Spitfire marks, rather than a conventional sliding canopy, to maintain airtight pressurisation the canopy had to be locked in place – though in an emergency it could be jettisoned in flight with small explosive charges.

Officially designated the Mk VI, the first prototype (R7120) was completed in June 1941. A second prototype (X4942) followed shortly after. This one differed from the original prototype in having distinctive pointed, extended wingtips, which all production Mk VIs would feature. Both R7120 and X4942 were sent to the A & AEE's High Altitude Flight at Boscombe Down for testing. Initially equipped with a pair of Spitfires and four Hurricanes, the High Altitude Flight had been formed in December 1940, with the job of testing aircraft at very high altitudes and developing solutions to the problems flying at extreme heights presented, including windscreen fogging and stability issues. Among the Flight's test pilots was Maurice 'Shorty' Longbottom, who conducted dozens of flights up to 40,000ft in a specially lightened Spitfire Mk II. Such experimental flying was, of course, extremely hazardous and fatal crashes were not uncommon.

The second prototype, X4942, flew first, on 4 July 1941, with the famed Spitfire test pilot Jeffrey Quill at the controls, while R7120 didn't make its maiden flight until 25 August. Flight trials found that the top speed of the Mk VI was 356 mph at 21,800ft but that this dropped to 264 mph when it reached its ceiling of 39,200ft. Numerous problems were also identified when flying at such an altitude. Among these were leakage of oil mist into the cockpit from the compressor and stiffness of the controls, while longitudinal stability at high altitude was also judged to be poor. More serious still was the fact that most of the 84 gallons of fuel carried in the tanks was used up in the climb to maximum altitude, which took over thirty minutes, leaving the pilot with virtually no time to locate and engage the enemy.

Despite these drawbacks, with the need for the high-altitude Spitfire considered pressing, the Air Ministry went ahead with an order for 100 Mk VIs, with an eventual total of ninety-eight being delivered between January and November 1942.

On 23 May 1942 a production Mk VI (BR289) was sent to Duxford to undergo intensive evaluation by the Air Fighting Development Unit. 'Numerous flights have been carried out between 30,000 and 37,500ft and the pilot has greatly benefited from the pressure cabin. There have been no complaints of ill-effects from being at altitude, even for long periods,' the AFDU reported, although it was found that hot air entering the cockpit from the cabin blower 'makes the cockpit uncomfortably warm and at altitudes below 15,000ft pilots felt muzzy and sleepy ... On one occasion on a particularly hot day, the temperature at low altitude inside the cockpit was almost unbearable.'[5]

On the second test flight 'cracks in the Perspex behind the hood appeared'. These were sealed with Bostik glue which, the report's author noted, 'was not altogether satisfactory'. The highest altitude reached during the trials was 37,500ft. However, 'at this height excessive hunting and intermittent cutting out of the engine was experienced due to the petrol vaporising in the feed line due to insufficient fuel pressure. On a very hot day (28°C on the ground) it was impossible to climb above 28,500ft due to this trouble.' In comparison flights against a Mk Vb, it was discovered that the Mk VI 'is more manoeuvrable than the Spitfire VB above 30,000ft'.[6]

To increase performance, later that year the Mk VI's Merlin engine was modified to use an experimental liquid oxygen injection system, which raised the ceiling by another 2,000ft and maximum speed by a further 50 mph. But the liquid oxygen was felt to be too volatile for combat and the system was not installed in operational aircraft.

Pilots who flew the type operationally were, on the whole, unimpressed, with the sealed canopy being singled out for particular criticism. Wing Commander Pete Brothers, a Battle of Britain ace who flew the Spitfire VI at RAF Skeabrae in the Orkneys in the autumn of 1942 – tasked with defending the Scapa Flow naval base from German reconnaissance aircraft – said:

> With the Mk VI the groundcrew literally screwed you into the cockpit in order to preserve the aircraft's pressurisation. Up at high altitude, the fighter became very stiff on the ailerons and elevators, and once we realised that the Ju 86P flights had all but ceased we took all the pressure seals out, removed the high altitude wing tips, and thus created a clipped-wing Mk VI, which we used to great effect at low-level! We never bothered to return them back to their original configuration, thus leaving these machines in essentially a Mk V fit.[7]

The first squadron to be equipped with the Mk VI was No 616 in April 1942, which was based at RAF Kings Cliffe in Northamptonshire, where its main roles were defence against hit-and-run Luftwaffe raiders and fighter sweeps over northern France. On the 2nd, the squadron's pilots and ground crew personnel were sent to Boscombe Down to learn about the new model and began operations with the type the following month. They carried out their first operational sortie on 9 May, when two of the squadron's Mk VIs and ten Mk Vbs took part in an uneventful fighter sweep over the French coast, accompanied by more Mk Vbs of No 411 Sqn. On the 25th, the Mk VI was involved in air combat for the first time during a scramble in which a lone Dornier Do 217 bomber was intercepted and attacked over the Leicester area, the squadron's ORB reporting:

> Three of our aircraft fired and return fire was experienced from the upper dorsal turret. Unfortunately, P/O Brown was hit in the right eye by a piece of Perspex, and despite the injury fired at the enemy. He made a perfect landing at North Luffenham and was rushed to hospital.[8]

Pilot Officer Brown lost his eye and, though damaged, the Do 217 escaped. The next day another of the squadron's pilots, New Zealander Pilot Officer Ware, was killed when his Mk VI crashed on a practice flight near RAF Scampton, witnesses stating that they saw his Spitfire go into a high-speed dive before hitting the ground.

By the beginning of June the squadron had been fully re-equipped with the Mk VI, and various issues with the type were by now manifesting themselves, chief among them being cockpit overheating below 20,000ft. Due to this, restrictions were imposed on operational flying below that height which, noted the squadron ORB, 'cut down operational activity considerably'.[9] In July came a temporary move to RAF Kenley for three weeks to take part in cross-Channel sweeps in conjunction with Mk Vb-equipped squadrons, though the ORB bemoaned the fact that their Spitfires 'could not be put to their proper use as high cover'. On the other hand, it was noted that by the end of the month 'most of the troubles connected with the pressure cabin had been overcome'.[10]

July 1942 also saw No 124 Sqn exchange its Mk Vbs for Mk VIs, although like the pilots of No 616 they 'do not take to them very much for various reasons'.[11] On 30 July the two squadrons joined forces to form 'a Spitfire VI wing' on cross-Channel fighter sweeps. At this time the RAF was struggling to deal effectively with the Luftwaffe's new Focke-Wulf Fw 190, which outperformed the Spitfire Mk V in almost all respects. No 616's Mk VIs had their first encounter with this formidable German fighter while on a sweep to Calais on 30 July, when they were bounced by a mixed force of around fifty Fw 190s and Bf 109s. The Mk VI proved no more effective against the Focke-Wulf than the Mk V on this occasion, losing four aircraft in the clash, with two pilots killed.

There were more clashes between No 616 and 124 Sqn's Mk VIs and the Fw 190 in August, in the epic air battles which took place during the ill-fated Anglo-Canadian landings at Dieppe on 19 July (Operation Jubilee). The pilots of No 124 claimed two Ju 88s and four Fw 190s as definitely or probably destroyed, and a further four Fw 190s damaged during the intense fighting. Operating from Hawkinge, No 616 claimed six Fw 190s damaged and a single Do 217 destroyed, for the loss of three of their own aircraft and one pilot. The Do 217 was shot down by the Australian ace Flying Officer Frederick 'Tony' Gaze, who ended the war with a DFC and two bars. But the Mk VIs deficiencies as a pure fighter were painfully exposed on 17 February 1943. Described by No 124 Sqn as 'a black day', four of their Spitfire VIs were shot down and all the pilots lost in a dogfight with over forty Fw 190s near Dunkirk.

Another duty added to the Mk VI-equipped squadrons from early September 1942 was providing high-level fighter escort for USAAF B-17 bombing raids over northern France. That month the Mk VI also finally saw action in the role for which it had originally been conceived, high altitude interception, when the type helped defend southern England against enemy raids carried out by the Ju 86R (see Chapter Eight). Once these raids had subsided, on 23 September No 616 made another move, this time to Tangmere, and was given the unexpected new task of countering the Luftwaffe's 'tip-and-run' raids – harassing attacks carried out on targets in the south-east of England by 'bombed-up' Fw 190 and Bf 109s at extremely low level. As the Squadron's ORB commented: 'As these patrols are all low down, they seem rather unsuited to high altitude fighters.'[12]

With the ongoing problem of trying to halt Ju 86R photo-reconnaissance flights over the Middle East and the Mediterranean, in October 1942 five Spitfire Mk VIs (BS106, BS124, BS133, BS134 and BS149) were shipped out to Egypt to join 103 Maintenance Unit's High Altitude Flight at Aboukir. But the Mk VI, largely thanks to the additional weight of the pressurised cockpit, was unable to match the altitude of the stripped-down Mk Vbs and IXs, which were by then beginning to enjoy some success against the Ju 86R, and they made little impact in this theatre.

Back in the UK, the Mk VI was used increasingly in attempts to intercept Ju 88D reconnaissance aircraft making PR runs over the south coast at high altitude, again without much success. No 616 was one of the squadrons assigned this task. 'During the month we had 15 scrambles, mainly against high-flying reconnaissance aircraft in the Portsmouth – Southampton area … but on Mk VI Spitfires, which are now mostly rather elderly machines, were unable to gain enough height to intercept,' the squadron ORB for August 1943 complained.[13]

Twelve Mk VIs were also deployed to northern Scotland, to supplement Mk Vbs operated by squadrons posted to the Orkneys and Shetlands, to ward off occasional high-altitude German recce flights by aircraft based in Norway to photograph Scapa Flow. No 602 Sqn, under the command of Wing Commander Brothers, was the first unit to operate the Mk VI in Scotland, the squadron arriving in September 1942 and being split between Skeabrae in the Orkneys and Sumburgh in the Shetlands. At the end of November No 129 Sqn arrived to relieve them and took over No 602's Mk VIs, 'of which,' the Squadron's ORB commented, 'we were pleased to see the last'.[14] Nor did the pilots of No 129 much care for their new mount, considering them 'inferior aeroplanes compared with the Spitfire Vb'.[15] Like their counterparts in No 602, No 129's time in the Orkneys was uneventful, with only occasional scrambles – usually false alarms – and no interceptions of enemy high flyers. In January 1943 No 129 Sqn passed on their Mk VIs in turn to No 234 Sqn, who were based at RAF Grimsetter in Kirkwall.

Another user of the Mk VI, albeit relatively briefly, was No 310 (Czech) Sqn, during its posting to Castletown in Caithness. Again, enemy activity was scarce and their only loss came on 27 August 1943 when the CO's car crashed into one of their Mk VIs while it was taxiing out of the aircraft pen.

The improved Mk VII

Overall, the Spitfire Mk VI cannot be regarded as a great success, and the remaining examples were phased out of frontline service during the latter part of 1943. Its shortcomings were well recognised by the RAF, prompting the development of an improved pressurised Spitfire to address these faults, even as the Mk VI was entering squadron service. The resultant Mk VII would be a far more successful aircraft.

Like its predecessor, the Mk VII also featured extended, pointed wingtips to improve the rate of climb and increase the ceiling. But it was fitted with a more powerful Merlin 64 engine, producing 1,710 hp and giving it a top speed of 408 mph at 25,000ft. The airframe was strengthened and it was also the first production Spitfire to incorporate a retractable tailwheel. To remedy one of the major weaknesses of the Mk VI, its lack of endurance, the Mk VII had an enlarged fuselage tank with a capacity of 96 gallons, and two additional wing tanks, each carrying 12.75 gallons. It could also carry an auxiliary belly tank to further extend its range. But the biggest improvement was the pressurised cockpit, which now had a conventional sliding canopy. A total of 141 Mk VIIs were built, and it made its first flight in April 1942. Testing was carried out by Boscombe Down's High Altitude Flight in August on the prototype Mk VII (AB450), where it was established that with reduced armament and armour it could reach 44,000ft, and at 40,000ft had a top speed of 400 mph. In the summer of 1944 one Mk VII was fitted with a Merlin 71 engine. This experimental aircraft had a service ceiling of just over 45,000ft.[16]

In contrast to the Mk VI, this new pressurised Spitfire was warmly received by the men who flew it. Flying Officer Don Nicholson of No 131 Sqn said:

> The Mk VII was designed for high-altitude operations and our planes wore high-altitude camouflage, light grey on top and blue-grey underneath. I liked the Mk VII. It was a good aeroplane. The highest I ever took one was to 39,000ft; it could have continued climbing, but I had no reason to go any higher.[17]

Another pilot who flew the type in combat, Pilot Officer Ian Blair, described the Mk VII as 'phenomenal', while Wing Commander Brothers, who operated the Mk VII on sorties over Occupied Europe, appreciated its great range, which 'allowed us to sweep as far east over the Continent as the Swiss border'.[18]

Several were attached to the Special Service Flight at Northolt, comprising pilots specially trained in high-altitude operations. The Special Service Flight was absorbed into No 124 Sqn at North Weald in January 1943, bringing with them 'lots of very useful experience … and some of the new VIIs, with which the Squadron will be re-equipped'.[19] As it had been doing with the Mk VI, No 124's main task was intercepting enemy intruders sneaking in at high altitude, though such occurrences were rare. From September 1943 the squadron also began flying 'Ramrods' – escort missions for bombers raiding targets in France, intended to draw German fighters into combat. During these missions the Mk VII demonstrated its worth as a fighter, shooting down a Bf 109 near Cherbourg on 9 September, an Fw 190 claimed as a probable over the Channel on 3 October, and a pair of Bf 109s on 14 February 1944 off Cap Griz-Nez and Sangatte. One of the pilots involved in the latter combat, Flight Sergeant Kelly, described the action:

> I chased the e/a for about 10 minutes, weaving in and out of church spires and chimney stacks and saw a few bursts from the occasional flak tower. I was now getting +18 boost and having closed to about 600 yards I fired several short bursts of cannon and m/g from dead line astern and saw a cannon strike on the port wing of the e/a. This succeeded in slowing up the e/a. I fired several more short bursts from line astern from about 500 yards and saw more strikes. My port cannon and m/g had a stoppage. I was now closing to within good range of the e/a which was leading me over towns and once I nearly lost it in a thick industrial haze. The e/a tried to lose me by steep turning on the deck round rising ground and chimneys. We passed over an airfield but no a/c or activity was apparent. I had now closed to 75 yards and recognised e/a as a Me 109 and with my starboard m/g (the starboard cannon had a stoppage caused by excessive banking) I gave the e/a a further burst – the e/a streamed white smoke which covered my windscreen and pulling up to 500ft the e/a's hood flew off and the pilot was seen to bale out, his parachute opening. To avoid hitting the machine I did a steep turn and did not see the e/a crash.[20]

From August 1943, No 616 Squadron based at RAF Ibsley in Hampshire began converting from the unloved Mk VI to the Mk VII, receiving its first example on the 29th, which was 'a cause of great rejoicing in the Squadron'.[21] As with No 124, their duties included interception of occasional intruders, bomber escort and offensive sweeps over northern France.

A third squadron, No 131, became operational with the Mk VII in March 1944 and the next month joined No 616 and several other units to form the 'Culmhead Wing', whose main task was to attack targets in the Normandy area in the run-up to and after Operation Overlord. 'On these missions we hit anything that took our fancy – vehicles, trains and airfields, mostly … We would patrol over France at 6,000ft, in order to be above the light flak, and generally look out for trains and other targets,' explained Wing Commander Brothers. Another mission assigned to the Mk VII-equipped squadrons was providing escort to bombers mounting attacks on 'Noball' sites – the codeword for targets associated with the V1 'doodlebug' flying bomb, particularly their 'ski jump' launch ramps, in the Pas de Calais area. 'The Spit VII was a favourite for these sweeps due to its range,' revealed Brothers.[22]

In the summer of 1944 No 124 began exchanging its Mk VIIs for IXs, its final sortie with the VII being a 'Ramrod' mission, escorting Lancaster and Halifax bombers on a raid on Caen on 18 July. That month No 616 also gave up its Mk VIIs to become the first squadron to equip with the new Gloster Meteor jet fighter, which it used on 'Diver' patrols – the interception of V1 flying bombs heading for London. In addition, as had been the case with the Mk VI, several Mk VIIs were assigned to the

Station Flight at RAF Skeabrae, at the disposal of squadrons sent north to the Orkneys for a period of rest.

No 154 Sqn at Biggin Hill would be the final fighter unit to equip with the Mk VII, using them as bomber escorts from November 1944 until February 1945, when it was withdrawn from frontline service. Several, however, would continue in service conducting meteorological work with No 1402 Flight and Nos 518 and 519 Squadrons until the end of the war.

Photo-recce 'Strato Spits'

Just as the Luftwaffe had demonstrated with the Ju 86P that pressurised aircraft flying at altitudes of 40,000ft or more could carry out reconnaissance over well-defended enemy airspace with something approaching impunity, inevitably the British also developed specialised variants of the Spitfire with pressurisation for high-altitude PR work.

Upon the outbreak of war the RAF relied mainly on a modified version of its twin-engine Bristol Blenheim bomber for photo-reconnaissance. But as the Germans had found with the Do 17 and He 111, such aircraft were not ideal for the purpose, proving much too vulnerable to fighter interception. The inadequacy of the aircraft available for PR work was recognised even before the war by some far-sighted officers in the RAF. One of these was Flight Lieutenant Maurice 'Shorty' Longbottom (later to become a distinguished test pilot at Boscombe Down's High Altitude Flight). In a paper he submitted to the Air Ministry in August 1939, *Photographic Reconnaissance of Enemy Territory in War*, Longbottom argued that rather than use twin-engine machines like the Blenheim, the task would be better suited to:

> a single, small machine, relying solely on its speed, climb and ceiling to avoid detection ... In clear weather the aircraft would fly at a great height all the time it was over enemy territory ... and with its great speed and advantage of height it could almost certainly elude fighters coming up to intercept it.[23]

The Spitfire was the obvious candidate.

But Air Chief Marshal Sir Hugh Dowding was loath to release any of his precious Spitfires for duties other than air defence. Nevertheless, in October 1939 he grudgingly agreed to hand over a pair of Spitfire Mk Is to the 'Heston Flight' – so called because it was located at Heston airfield near London – which had been formed by the Australian businessman and aviator Sidney Cotton, who used civilian-registered aircraft to carry out covert photography of Germany on behalf of MI6 from February 1939. Designated the PR.Mk IA, they were equipped with two Fairchild F.24 vertical cameras installed in the wings in place of the Browning machine-guns, had their radios removed and were painted in a pale green colour scheme, known as 'camotint'. So modified, they could now fly around 12 mph faster than the standard fighter version of the Spitfire.

Given the cover name No 2 Camouflage Unit, the two aircraft deployed to Séclin in northern France in November 1939. Flying Spitfire N3071, Flight Lieutenant Longbottom (who had been seconded to the 'Heston Flight' in September), carried out the

Spitfire's first operational PR sortie on 18 November, flying at 33,000ft over the German-Belgian border to photograph enemy fortifications around the city of Aachen – though a navigation error led to him photographing the Belgian border city of Eupen by mistake. Still, the flight proved the point – Longbottom made it back safely to Séclin with his photographs, unmolested by Luftwaffe fighters. In the following weeks, several more successful Spitfire PR flights over Germany were carried out, with no losses. In January 1940 the unit's cover designation was dropped, becoming the Photographic Development Unit, and in March, Flight Lieutenant Longbottom's work with the unit was recognised with the award of a DFC.

Some in the Air Ministry, however, insisted the high-altitude photography taken by the new unit lacked sufficient detail to be of much military value. The ever-resourceful Cotton convinced them otherwise by enlisting civilian experts from an aerial survey company, who with the aid of the latest 3D stereoscopic equipment were able to interpret the photographs and successfully identify military targets.

With the Spitfire's suitability for reconnaissance work proven beyond doubt, a dozen more were allocated for the task and a second Spitfire PR unit, No 212 Squadron, was formed at Meaux in France. Although a great improvement over the RAF's converted bombers, that PR Spitfires were not immune to interception was shown on 22 March 1940, when one was shot down by a Bf 109 over Kleve, killing its pilot, Pilot Office Clive Wheatley.

After the fall of France, in June the PDU received another change of title, to the Photographic Reconnaissance Unit, and a change of location in December, to RAF Benson in Oxfordshire, felt to be less vulnerable to enemy attack after Heston was bombed by the Luftwaffe in September, destroying several of their Spitfires.

Forced now to operate from UK bases, increasing the range of the PR Spitfire became a priority. This led to the development of several new versions with longer 'legs'. In November 1940 the PR.Mk ID – or 'super extra-long range' version – entered service with the PRU, whose enlarged wing fuel tanks had a capacity of 114 gallons, allowing it to reach deep into Germany from bases in eastern England. Carrying out flights lasting several hours, a doctor was based at Benson to assess the physiological effects on the PRU's pilots of their long high-altitude sorties.

The capabilities of the RAF's PR Spitfires continued to improve as the war went on, and served as the Allies' most important 'eye in the sky'. During 1942, however, the introduction of new German fighters, the Fw 190 and the Bf 109G model, often equipped with the GM-1 nitrous oxide power boost system to improve performance at high altitude, led to a worrying increase in the losses of PR Spitfires over Germany, prompting efforts to further improve the ceiling of the Spitfire in the next PR model, the Mark XI. Based on the Mk VIII airframe and powered by the Merlin 61 engine, the Spitfire PR.Mk XI had a top speed of 417 mph and was capable of reaching 42,000ft. Carrying over 200 gallons of fuel in its wing and fuselage tanks, it also boasted an impressive range of 1,360 miles. With 471 built, the Mk XI was produced in greater numbers than any other PR Spitfire variant.

The PR.Mk XI entered service with No 541 Squadron in December 1942, and soon wrested back the initiative from the Luftwaffe. The PR.Mk XI's lack of a pressurised cockpit, however, could leave the pilot susceptible to the effects of the 'bends' on long-range, high-altitude flights, as one airman from No 541 discovered on a sortie to photograph Berlin on 20 December 1943. 'While at 40,000ft over Berlin the pilot had a severe attack of bends in the left arm and leg but relieved it to some extent by turning on his emergency oxygen,' the Squadron's ORB reported.[24] Another problem regularly experienced by the pilots was frost forming on the inside of the cockpit canopy. 'Various expedients have been tried to keep the inside of the hood free from frost, but so far without complete success.'[25]

New Zealander Flight Lieutenant Whaley of No 541 Squadron had reason to be thankful for the high ceiling of his PR.Mk XI during a sortie on 24 May 1944 to photograph the port of Cherbourg, as the Squadron's ORB revealed:

> While near Cherbourg he was chased by two enemy aircraft, probably FW 190, and 5 separate attacks were made. When he first noticed them he was at 28,000 [ft] but evaded them by making steep climbing turns to 40,000. The hostile aircraft followed up to about 38,000 but in no case got within about 1000 yds range.[26]

Besides the RAF, the 14th Photographic Squadron of the USAAF's 7th Photographic Reconnaissance Group, based at Mount Farm airfield in Oxfordshire, was also equipped with a number of PR.Mk XIs for long-range photo-reconnaissance missions over Occupied Europe. On 6 March 1944, Major Walter Weitner of the 7th PRG carried out the USAAF's first PR sortie to Berlin in a PR.Mk XI, nicknamed 'High Lady', to photograph the results of an air raid by bombers of the US Eighth Air Force. Approaching Berlin at 39,000ft, his position was betrayed by the white contrails left by his Spitfire in the cold air at such high altitude. Through the rear-view mirror fixed to his canopy he saw three Bf 109Gs pursuing him. Flying at 360 mph, the American climbed to 41,500ft, beyond the ceiling of his pursuers. 'Gradually the German fighters began to fall back and finally the last slid from view,' he recalled.[27] The rest of the mission was uneventful, Weitner successfully photographing the target and landing safely back at Mount Farm, his fuel tanks virtually dry, after a flight lasting a total of four hours and eighteen minutes. For this sortie Major Weitner was awarded the Silver Star.

Pressurised Spitfires were first used in the PR role in spring 1943, when several of the Mk VIs sent to Aboukir to help combat the Ju 86R spy flights over the Middle East and Mediterranean were modified by 103 MU, with the installation of an F.8 camera in the fuselage. During April and May they operated briefly over Crete and mainland Greece. A dedicated pressurised PR Spitfire followed in early 1944. Designated the PR.Mk X, it combined the Mk VII fighter's pressurised cockpit and airframe with the wings of the PR.Mk XI. From April 1944 this variant partially equipped No 541 and 542 Squadrons, flying its first missions in May. Considered an interim type pending the introduction of the superior PR.Mk XIX, the Mk X was not popular with those who flew it, the poor view through the thick Perspex canopy being a major complaint. Only sixteen examples of this mark were produced.

Regarded as the ultimate PR Spitfire, the Mk XIX was fitted with the more powerful Griffon 65 engine, making it the fastest of all the Spitfire marks, with a top speed of 442 mph and a ceiling of 44,000ft.[28] With a total fuel capacity in its internal tanks of 252 gallons (which could be supplemented by either a 90 or 170 gallon drop tank), it also boasted the greatest range of any Spitfire, at 1,550 miles. The camera installation typically comprised either a single or a pair of the new F.52 vertical cameras, which offered greater definition photographs taken at high-altitude, fitted in the fuselage behind the cockpit, and a single F.24 for oblique photography. No 541 Squadron was the first to receive the type, in May 1944. The Mk XIX continued in service with the RAF after the war, carrying out its last operational sortie – photographing suspected Communist guerrilla positions in Malaya – in April 1954.

Along with the pressurised Mosquito PR.Mk XVI (which was also used by the US Eighth Air Force, known in USAAF service as the F8), the Mk XIX was the RAF's most important long-range reconnaissance platform during the latter part of the Second World War, and proved almost immune from interception. On one occasion, the unarmed PR aircraft even managed to achieve a 'kill'. While on a PR flight over the Rhine on 6 October 1944 in his Mk XIX, Flight Lieutenant Richard Garvey of No 541 Squadron was attacked by a pair of Fw 190s. To shake off his pursuers Garvey put the Spitfire into a tight spiral dive, pulling out at near zero feet. One of his attackers followed him down but failed to pull out in time and crashed into a wooded area. This, stated the combat report, was 'one of the few instances of unarmed aircraft being responsible for the destruction of hostile huns'.[29] Flight Lieutenant Garvey was awarded a bar to his DFC for this exploit, the citation stating: 'This incident is characteristic of the skill and determination consistently displayed by this officer.'

Goering was furious at the PR Spitfires' ability to penetrate German airspace in daylight with near impunity. 'It is amazing how the Spitfire flies so high, with its cameras, beyond Koln and Frankfurt. They have become a great hindrance,' he fumed.[30] Only with the introduction into Luftwaffe service of the Messerschmitt Me 262 jet fighter in the summer of 1944 was the PR Spitfire's virtual immunity from interception seriously challenged. Flight Lieutenant Jimmy Taylor, who flew Spitfire PR.Mk XIs with No 16 Squadron, described the threat posed by the enemy jets:

> We felt we could outfly and outrun the usual enemy fighters, but the German jets were just coming into operation, and because they were always vastly outnumbered by Allied fighters, they regarded the solitary high-flying spy planes as fair game. But their duration was short and we reckoned we could outmanoeuvre them until they had to go home.[31]

Chapter Six

Replacing the Ju 86R

C hased out of Mediterranean skies by the Desert Air Force's Spitfires, by mid-1943 the only theatre where the Ju 86R still enjoyed immunity from interception was the Eastern Front, where the Soviet Air Force's lack of fighters capable of operating at very high altitudes was now emerging as a serious deficiency. Since summer 1942 reconnaissance flights by Ju 86Rs over Moscow had been a particular nuisance to the Russians. In response, the Soviets developed high altitude versions of several of their most successful warplanes: the Petlyakov Pe-2, the Yak-9 and the MiG-3.

Designed by Vladimir Petlyakov in the late 1930s, the Pe-2 was originally conceived as a high-altitude fighter before evolving into a multi-role aircraft – essentially the Soviet equivalent of the de Havilland Mosquito – which served as a level and dive-bomber, heavy fighter, night-fighter, ground-attack and reconnaissance aircraft. A requirement for a high-altitude interceptor version, designated the Pe-2 VI (*Vysotnyi Istrebitel* – High Altitude Fighter) was reinstated in 1941, but the Nazi invasion in the summer forced work on this variant to be suspended as all development and production effort was directed towards essential types. In late 1942, however, the Pe-2 VI project was revived and three prototypes were ordered. The first test flight took place on 30 April 1943, but severe misting of the cockpit was encountered by the test pilot at altitude. A second test flight a few days later ended with the pilot making an emergency landing due to engine failure. These and other technical problems led to the Pe-2 VI's cancellation soon after.

Another attempt to adapt a proven type to deal with the Ju 86R was the Yak-9PD. Introduced in 1942, the Yak-9 was the most widely produced Soviet fighter of the war, with almost 17,000 of all versions rolling off the production lines. Work commenced on the Yak- 9PD high-altitude variant in November 1942. The main differences with the standard fighter were the replacement of the Klimov M-105 engine with the improved M-105PD unit, and the removal of the two 12.7mm machine-guns, leaving the single ShVak 20mm cannon housed in the propeller hub as its only armament. The first of five prototypes was delivered in April 1943 to the 12th Guards IAP (Fighter Aviation Regiment) for testing under operational conditions. But the initial flights revealed numerous problems, not least overheating of the engine during the long climb to altitude and a maximum ceiling of just 38,220ft.

Despite these deficiencies, attempts were made to intercept the Ju 86Rs that were still roving over the capital unchallenged using the Yak-9PD. On 2 June 1943 Lieutenant Colonel Sholokhov was scrambled in one of the prototypes from the Khodynka air base in response to an intruder flying at 41,000ft over Moscow. While climbing, the Yak's water temperature reached 105°C and the oil temperature 95°C. Eventually, after reaching the aircraft's maximum altitude over the outskirts of Moscow, Sholokhov spotted a Ju 86R around 3,000–5,000ft above him. But then the oil pressure suddenly plummeted.

After descending 3,000ft he made a second attempt to intercept the Junkers, but at a height of 37,400ft steam began to pour from the engine and the cockpit windshield iced over, forcing him to abandon the chase and land back at base.

There were more attempts to intercept Ju 86Rs during the summer. Several Yak-9PDs were again scrambled on the morning of 22 August 1943 when another Ju 86R was detected flying over Moscow. The German snooper loitered for around an hour and a half photographing the city and the surrounding area, but the Yaks were unable to reach his altitude. The next day the commander of the capital's air defences, General Mikhail Gromadin, complained in a report that the problem of providing high-altitude fighter defence for Moscow had yet to be resolved.

Improvements were made to the Yak-9PD. The wing span was increased, weight was further reduced and a new engine, the Klimov M-106PV, with water injection and greater high-altitude performance was fitted. Engineers also addressed the problem of engine overheating during the climb to altitude by making improvements to the coolant system. These changes allowed the new improved version of the Yak-9PD to reach an altitude of 45,280ft during flight tests in 1944 and a small number were ordered into production. But by then the need for a specialised high-altitude interceptor had passed.

The third Soviet high-altitude interceptor project was a series of prototypes based on another workhorse of the PVO's fighter force: the MiG-3. Entering service in early 1941, the MiG-3, along with the obsolescent Polikarpov I-15, I-153 and I-16, bore the brunt of the early fighting on the Eastern Front. Distinguished by its very long nose which accommodated a

Mikulin AM-35 inline engine, the MiG-3 had originally been designed as a high-altitude interceptor, making it poorly suited to the low-level air combat that prevailed on the Eastern Front. Consequently, losses were high. Several attempts were made to adapt the MiG for extreme altitude operations, beginning with the I-210, which swapped the AM-35 for a Shvetsov M-82 radial engine. Although this proved a failure, development work continued with the I-211 and I-220. The service ceiling of these, however, still fell well below that of the Ju 86R.

The MiG design bureau persevered with the I-221 (which added a turbo-supercharger), I-222 (incorporating a pressurised cockpit) and I-224. Much more impressive heights of between 46,200 and 47,500ft were achieved in flight trials conducted during 1944 in these aircraft, but by that time enemy high-altitude reconnaissance flights had dwindled and so no production orders were forthcoming.

As in the Mediterranean, it was the Spitfire that apparently finally brought the Ju 86R spy flights to an end on the Eastern Front. The Soviet Air Force's introduction to Britain's most illustrious fighter came in March 1941, when the Germans – then still allies of Stalin – invited Soviet test pilot Stepan Suprun to fly a captured RAF Spitfire Mk I in Germany.[1] After the launch of Operation Barbarossa three months later, Stalin turned to his new British ally to replace the catastrophic losses his air force had suffered in the opening days of the Nazi invasion. Churchill responded by sending Hawker Hurricane Mk IIBs to the Soviets.

But it was the Spitfire that the Soviets really wanted. Several Spitfire PR.IVs which the RAF had used to conduct reconnaissance flights from Vaenga near Murmansk in autumn 1942, photographing German warships in Norwegian waters, were handed over to the Soviets and used by the Northern Fleet. Following a plea from Stalin in October 1942, Churchill agreed to send 143 refurbished former RAF Spitfire Vbs, the first batch of thirty-five being shipped to Basra aboard the *City of Derby* in early 1943, from where they were ferried to Azerbaijan via Iran. Repainted with the red star, the Soviet Spitfires first saw action with the 57th Guards IAP over the Kuban bridgehead in April 1943.

That summer twenty Spitfire Vbs were allocated to the defence of Moscow, serving with the 16th and 67th Guards IAPs. Along with the Yak-9PDs, two took part in the attempt on 22 August 1943 to intercept the Ju 86R over the capital. Senior Lieutenant Semonov managed to get up to 37,700ft, around 1,600ft below and 650ft behind the Ju 86R, but after a few short bursts his guns froze and the German escaped. Another intercept by a Spitfire two weeks later also ended in disappointment when the pilot, Junior Lieutenant Zernov, ran out of oxygen during the climb to altitude, forcing him to break off the chase.

However, there was a claim of a Ju 86R being brought down by a Spitfire over Moscow on 15 October 1943, though this has never been confirmed. In any case, the arrival of the Spitfires and the ever-strengthening Soviet air defences convinced Luftwaffe commanders that the Ju 86R's time was up and the few surviving examples were withdrawn from frontline service soon after.

The difficulties the Luftwaffe was now experiencing in gaining reconnaissance of Russian positions were revealed in an October 1943 signal from I *Fliegerkorps*, decrypted by the codebreakers at Bletchley Park, which admitted: 'For some time it has been impossible to reconnoitre enemy bases in the south-eastern Black Sea owing to too strong defences.'[2]

A new Ju 86R

From that point on, Luftwaffe reconnaissance on all the fronts fell into rapid decline, with disastrous consequences for the German war effort, as the RLM struggled to find a suitable replacement for the Ju 86R. Junkers proposed an improved version of its high-flyer, designated the R-3 model. This would've been the ultimate incarnation of the Ju 86R, with a projected ceiling of 52,000ft. It was to be powered by the new Jumo 208 engine, work on which had begun in 1939. But development problems led to the cancellation of the Jumo 208 and with it the Ju 86R-3. The same fate befell another, similar high-altitude Junkers project, the Ju 186, which was to have been powered by four Jumo 208 engines.

One type that did at least reach the prototype stage was the Dornier Do 217P, a pressurised variant of the Do 217 bomber. Closely resembling the earlier Do 17, the 217 was a larger aircraft, with increased range and bombload. After a difficult development, needlessly complicated by the RLM's initial insistence that the type be capable of dive-bombing, an effective warplane eventually emerged. Entering service in early

1941, it served as a conventional level bomber – in which role it was used during the Baedeker raids of 1942 and Operation Steinbock in 1944 (the so-called 'Little Blitz') – night-fighter and anti-shipping strike aircraft, armed with cutting-edge stand-off weapons like the Fritz-X and Henschel Hs 293 radio-controlled missiles.

The Do 217's use in the reconnaissance role dated back to late 1940, when several pre-production aircraft were assigned to the *Kommando* Rowehl to assist the Ju 86Ps in the task of photographing Russian positions and defences prior to Operation Barbarossa. The Do 217P was a heavily modified version with a fully pressurised cabin in a redesigned nose and powered by two DB 603B supercharged engines, with an intercooler and two stage supercharger driven by a third engine, a DB 605T, installed in the rear of the fuselage. Several prototypes were built, the first making its maiden flight on 6 June 1942, during which it reached 37,000ft. Modifications were made, including extending the wingspan, and further test flights carried out over the following months, the test aircraft reaching an altitude of 49,800ft before the flight had to be abandoned due to stability problems. Development continued at a slow pace until the project was eventually discontinued owing to the worsening war situation. Two of the prototypes were destroyed in an Allied bombing raid on 5 September 1944.

As a stop-gap measure, the Luftwaffe turned to the Arado Ar 240. This twin-engine machine had begun life in 1938 as a potential successor to the Messerschmitt Bf 110 heavy fighter, or *zerstörer*. A combination of serious handling problems and the Luftwaffe's confidence in the *zerstörer* concept being severely shaken by the Bf 110's poor showing in the Battle of Britain (where it proved almost as vulnerable to RAF fighters as the bombers it was supposed to protect) limited production to a handful of prototypes. However, its impressive top speed (410 mph, with the aid of GM-1 nitrous oxide power boost) and cockpit pressurisation led to its adaptation for reconnaissance work. Three of the prototypes were stripped of armament, fitted with cameras and handed over to a unit at Orly to conduct PR runs over England from late 1943. 'Regular reconnaissance aircraft were then unable to bring back many pictures from England. The defences were too strong,' explained Oberleutnant Horst Goetz, one of the Luftwaffe pilots who flew the Ar 240 from Orly.

Goetz made multiple attempts to photograph the UK, all of them unsuccessful. 'We tried to fly over England with the Ar 240, but I always had to turn back because of the strong fighter defences. As we approached our "colleagues" were always waiting for us at a higher altitude,' he said.[3]

In the absence of suitable new types, the Luftwaffe's reconnaissance arm was forced to rely on established types like the Junkers Ju 88 to fulfil commanders' insatiable demands for aerial photography.

The hugely versatile Ju 88 had been used for reconnaissance, in the form of the D-1 and D-2 models, since the summer of 1940, equipped with Rb 50/30 high-altitude and Rb 20/30 low-altitude cameras. To improve the type's high-altitude performance, the GM-1 boost system was installed. Further improvements led to the Ju 88T, of which only a small number were built. Based on the airframe of the Ju 88S and powered by two BMW 801 radial engines, with the GM-1 system it had a maximum speed of 410 mph. Nevertheless, the Ju 88T also proved vulnerable over British skies. On 20 April 1943 a Ju 88T was on a PR sortie over south-east England when it was intercepted at a height of 36,000ft by a pair of Spitfire IXbs of No 332 (Norwegian) Squadron. The combat report stated:

> Blue 1 went into attack closing 250 yards from astern, giving a one second burst with cannon and m/gs which set the port engine on fire. After another burst pieces fell off the e/a. A third burst resulted in e/a turning over on its back and exploding. One of the crew was seen to bale out and he waved as our fighters circled him. From a statement given by one of the crew who baled out from this Ju 88, the attack delivered by Blue Section was a very good one.[4]

In mid-1943 the Junkers Ju 188 – essentially an improved Ju 88, with greater range and performance – began to enter squadron service with the Luftwaffe. Like the Ju 88 it fulfilled multiple roles, including reconnaissance. The Ju 188D-1 and D-2 were the standard recce types, powered by two Jumo 213 engines, and their high-altitude, high-speed performance allowed the Luftwaffe to regain a measure of the survivability enjoyed with the Ju 86R, especially over the Eastern Front. In October 1943 Luftwaffe commanders in southern Russia, who had been struggling to secure photographs of enemy positions with their existing aircraft, reported: 'Reconnaissance was today carried out for the first time with a new aircraft type JU 188 at an

altitude beyond the effective range of flak and of enemy fighters
… Heavy flak disintegrated 1,000 metres below the A/C.'[5] One
of those who flew the Ju 188 on PR sorties over the Eastern
Front was Oberleutnant Werner Muffey, who operated from
bases in Latvia and Poland. He recalled 'long and trouble-free
photo flights', and with the benefit of GM-1 he was able to avoid
Soviet fighters sent up to intercept.[6]

Besides the D model, a *Fernerkunder* variant, the F-1,
was also introduced, powered by the BMW 801 engine. But
Junkers believed the full potential of the airframe had yet to be
realised and a version with a pressurised cabin accommodating
a three-man crew, the Ju 188T, was put into development. This
project eventually matured into the Ju 388. Virtually identical
in appearance to the Ju 188, three versions of the Ju 388 – given
the name *Störtebeker* by Hitler, after a legendary fourteenth-
century German privateer – were planned: the 'J', 'K' and 'L'
models. All would be powered by BMW 801TJ air-cooled
turbo-supercharged engines, feature pressurised cabins and
be capable of operating at altitudes in excess of 40,000ft. The
'J' model was a night fighter, the 'K' was a bomber and the 'L'
was a long-range recce version, with an anticipated top speed of
385 mph at 38,000ft and a maximum range of 1,900 miles. One
interesting feature of the Ju 388 was the defensive armament,
which consisted of a remotely-controlled barbette in the tail,
housing two MG 131 machine-guns, with a periscopic sighting
mechanism above the cockpit for the crew to spot enemy fighters
approaching from behind.

A little over 100 examples were built, most of them the 'L'
variant, of which forty-seven reached frontline squadrons in the

last months of the war, but only a few operational sorties are believed to have been carried out before the German surrender. Several Ju 388Ls were captured intact by members of the USAAF's Air Intelligence unit (popularly known as 'Watson's Whizzers', after the unit's CO, Colonel Harold Watson) at the Merseburg air base in central Germany in May 1945. After initial examination, several were shipped back to the US along with many other captured German aircraft to be thoroughly evaluated by USAAF test pilots at Wright Field in Dayton, Ohio.

Though critical of the cramped crew compartment, the Americans were on the whole impressed with the machine. A report from the USAAF's Air Materiel Command, dated October 1946, stated:

> The Ju 388 was found to be quite manoeuvrable and it displayed desirable flying characteristics for its particular type. Although no aerobatics were attempted, it was evident that the airplane has a good rate of roll and a relatively short turning radius ... with one engine idling and the other at cruising power the Ju 388 has excellent single engine performance and handling characteristics.

The report concluded: 'An overall analysis of the airplane leads to the conclusion that it could be employed well in its design function of long-range reconnaissance.'[7]

Another reconnaissance project developed late in the war was the Hütter Hu 211. Designed by brothers Wolfgang and Ulrich Hütter, whose background was in glider design, the

Hu 211 was based on the airframe of Heinkel's He 219 *Uhu* ('Owl') night-fighter, and incorporated parts from the Ju 388 and Dornier's Do 335 fighter. With a wooden wing of 80ft span, it was intended to be powered by two Junkers Jumo 222 engines and have a ceiling of 52,000ft. In the event, the troubled Jumo 222 powerplant never reached full production and the two partially completed and engineless prototypes were destroyed in an air raid in early 1945.

The Germans even approached their Japanese ally about the possibility of acquiring the rights to manufacture their own version of the Mitsubishi Ki-46 reconnaissance aircraft, which boasted excellent high-altitude performance. But negotiations with Tokyo came to nothing.

With the failure of these projects and plans either to reach the production lines or enter operational service in time, in the mid-war period the Luftwaffe had no option but to soldier on with the Ju 88 and Ju 188 as its standard reconnaissance types, along with the Bf 109.

Reconnaissance had been a task undertaken by Nazi Germany's primary fighter since 1940, with the introduction of the Bf 109E-5 model, which had the two wing cannon removed and a vertical Rb 50/30 camera fitted in the fuselage behind the cockpit. This was followed by the Bf 109E-6 (differing only in that the armament it carried was stripped back further) and the E-9, which could carry a 66-gallon drop tank to extend the range. But the 109 still could not match the formidable endurance of the RAF's PR Spitfire.

By the time reconnaissance variants of the Bf 109G series had arrived in service, the maximum speed had increased to 426 mph and the ceiling to over 40,000ft, with the aid of the GM-1 system and MW-50 water-methanol injection in its DB 605 powerplant. Bf 109Gs based in northern France made regular recce sorties over southern England during 1943, relying on their speed and altitude to avoid the British defences. But the RAF's new Spitfire Mk VIIs proved a deadly obstacle.

From March 1943 No 124 Squadron maintained a 'High Flying Flight' of several of their new Mk VIIs at their North Weald base, with several more detached to RAF Exeter, held at a state of readiness 'for the purpose of the interception of any high-flying enemy aircraft which might come this way'.[8] The Flight had its first success on the afternoon of 15 May 1943, when a pair of Mk VIIs were scrambled from RAF Exeter in response to a Bf 109G on a suspected recce run near Plymouth. After climbing to 38,000ft the Spitfire pilots, Flying Officer Willis and Sergeant Wibberley, spotted condensation trails a thousand feet higher. Willis caught up with the Messerschmitt forty-five miles south-west of Start Point and opened fire at a range of 400 yards, seeing 'strikes and flashes from cockpit and wing roots'. As he prepared to make another attack, he 'saw pieces of the aircraft falling down and the pilot baling out'.[9] This is thought to have been the first confirmed 'kill' for the Spitfire Mk VII.

Over the next few months there were more shootdowns by Mk VIIs of Bf 109Gs on reconnaissance flights over southern England. On 13 June Warrant Officer Nowell shot down a 109G over the English Channel. Two days later the Under-Secretary of State for Air Lord Balfour paid a visit to the squadron and 'asked many technical questions regarding the high flying business and the intricacies of the [Spitfire] "Sevens" generally,' the Squadron ORB recorded.[10] Nowell scored another 'kill' on 26 June, bringing down a Bf 109G near Portsmouth, and on 16 August Flying Officer Brooks destroyed another at an altitude of 36,000ft off the Isle of Wight.

The 'Strato Spits' were also enjoying success against PR Bf 109s at the other end of the British Isles. In January 1944 No 602 (City of Glasgow) Squadron was sent to RAF Skeabrae in the Orkneys to defend the naval base at Scapa Flow from Bf 109Gs carrying out long-range reconnaissance sorties from Norway, equipped with auxiliary fuel tanks. For this task, the squadron had at its disposal three Spitfire Mk VIIs.

On 20 February 1944 British radar picked up a single contact heading towards the Orkneys at high altitude. Pilot Officer Ian Blair and Flight Lieutenant Bennetts, as Red 1 and 2, were scrambled in their Spitfire VIIs to investigate. Around fifty miles east of the Orkneys they spotted vapour trails and soon after the aircraft that had made them – a Bf 109G-6/R3 of the long-range reconnaissance squadron 1.(F)/120, based at Stavanger-Sola in southern Norway. The 109's pilot, Oberleutnant Helmut Quednau, turned away from the Spitfires and dived at high speed, Blair and Bennetts giving chase. 'At extreme range, Blair opened fire, but without results,' the Squadron ORB revealed. Bennetts went in to the attack but was forced to break off when his gunsight failed. Blair then carried out a second attack, this time with more success, as the ORB explained:

Blair immediately closed the range and at 200 yds or less fired a short burst. Well aimed indeed, for about 4ft of the Hun's starboard wing broke off and the e/a spun into the sea. On crashing into the sea it caught fire, and the pilot was not visible. Blair fired the telling burst when at approx. 4,000ft. The e/a was identified as a Messerschmitt 109, fitted with long range wing tanks which the German made no attempt to jettison.[11]

Oberleutnant Quednau was killed. Plt Off Blair did not escape from the clash unscathed, however. Debris from the Messerschmitt hit his radiator and coolant began to leak. He managed to nurse his damaged Spitfire back to the Orkneys and made a belly-landing in a peat bog on Stronsay Island, not far from RAF Skeabrae, with minor facial injuries. He was later collected and taken back to base in a Tiger Moth flown by one of his squadron mates, the Free French ace Pierre Clostermann.

Protecting Overlord

In the spring of 1944, the most important task assigned to the RAF's Air Defence of Great Britain (as Fighter Command had been renamed) was to prevent the Luftwaffe gaining photo-intelligence of the Allied invasion fleet assembling for Operation Overlord. The elaborate deception plan designed to convince Hitler that the Allies intended to invade at Pas de Calais rather than Normandy (Operation Fortitude) depended for its success on hiding the actual invasion preparations along England's south coast. This meant closing off the airspace around the invasion assembly ports to Luftwaffe reconnaissance. 'The Air

Marshal Commanding A.D.G.B. [Air Marshal Sir Roderic Hill] had reported that everything possible was being done to prevent these reconnaissances,' the Cabinet was informed on 2 May 1944, although Air Marshal Hill went on to warn that it would be 'difficult to guarantee that every single enemy aircraft would be intercepted before reaching these areas'.[12]

The Luftwaffe's fleet of reconnaissance aircraft in France mainly comprised Bf 109Gs, with some Ju 88Ds and Ju 188Ds, which made high-speed dashes over southern and eastern England at high altitude to provide the German High Command with a picture of Allied dispositions. But the airspace over each of the ports where the invasion fleet was assembling was protected by up to forty Spitfires, among them Mk VIIs, which maintained standing patrols in daytime. 'We were doing these high altitude patrols … to protect the southern part of the country – where we were preparing for the invasion – from being photographed by reconnaissance aircraft,' confirmed Flight Lieutenant Peter Ayerst, who flew Spitfire Mk VIIs with No 124 Squadron in 1944.[13]

The Bf 109Gs did, however, occasionally succeed in penetrating the fighter screen in the weeks leading up to D-Day and photographing the invasion ports, by making high-speed 'hit-and-run' sorties, at 39,000ft. But the Luftwaffe was able to provide only snapshots of the Allied build-up, not a comprehensive picture, 'on account of the lack of constant comprehensive air reconnaissance, the [enemy's] main transport effort in one sector or another of the Channel coast is not ascertainable', the Kriegsmarine complained on 22 May 1944.[14]

In the last days of May 1944 the Luftwaffe succeeded in bringing back photographs of just three of the harbours where the invasion fleet was gathering. The confusion among Germany's senior commanders over Allied intentions was revealed in a signal sent from Field Marshal Rommel's HQ to the C-in-C West, Field Marshal von Rundstedt, on the eve of D-Day: 'Air reconnaissance showed no great increase of landing-craft in Dover area. Other harbours of England's south coast NOT visited by reconnaissance aircraft ... Survey urgently needed of harbour moorings on the entire English south coast.'[15] And so the opportunity to detect the great Allied armada assembling to invade Normandy was missed, and with it Hitler's last realistic chance of winning the war.

When the landings did take place, overwhelming Allied air superiority ensured the German commanders received only a very fragmentary picture of what was unfolding at Normandy, with only one successful reconnaissance mission over the beaches being completed on D-Day itself – a high altitude dash by a pair of Bf 109G-8s. Ju 188D and F models and Bf 410s were also subsequently used to carry out high altitude reconnaissance of the beachheads by night, but these could not provide the detail required by OKW.

In desperation, the Luftwaffe pressed into service one of its new Bf 109H-1s. Originally intended as a specialised extreme altitude interceptor variant of the long-serving fighter, designed to meet a perceived threat from high-altitude Allied bombers (see Chapter Nine), it never operated in that role, but a few were converted for photo-reconnaissance. Based on the 109F airframe, the wingspan was increased from 32 to 39ft and it was to be fitted with the new DB 628 engine, an improved version of the DB 605 equipped with a two-stage supercharger. Test flights in late 1943 and early 1944 revealed some serious stability issues, but having reached an impressive altitude of 47,500ft in test flights it was felt the 109H-1 could survive in the skies over Normandy.

The British learned of the 109H's existence from the interrogation of a Bf 410 pilot shot down off the English coast in April 1944 and taken prisoner, who told his captors that 'a high altitude 109 with a wider wing than is normal was about to be put into operation [which] would attain a height of 13,500 metres'.[16]

In May, 5.(F)/123, a long-range reconnaissance squadron based at Monchy-Breton, received a single 109H from the Luftwaffe's maintenance and repair facility at Guyancourt, twenty miles west of Paris. After the Allied landings the following month, the squadron was ordered to use the new aircraft to photograph the northern French coastline, something the pilots felt was unrealistically ambitious. 'Those fools, the things they expected of the "H",' said Leutnant Walther Warthol, one of the squadron's pilots. 'They demanded a mosaic of the whole coast, from Cherbourg to the mouth of the Orne. That was supposed to be made on one flight.'

The unit's CO assured his men that the 109H's great height advantage would protect them from Allied fighters. But this did little to assuage the concerns of pilots like Warthol. 'We had to explain to him that we could get away for the moment by climbing, but we couldn't remain at a height of 14,200m, because we hadn't got the petrol for it,' he explained. 'The "H" has such a heavy consumption of petrol at high altitude that you can't keep it up. In the end the "H" has to come down again.'[17] Much to the relief of Leutnant Warthol and the other squadron pilots, soon after the unit's sole 109H was accidentally shot down by friendly flak while being flown by their CO, who survived a belly-landing.

In the end the Luftwaffe turned to its new jet-powered Arado Ar 234 to provide the photography the German army so desperately required during the Normandy fighting. With a top speed of 460 mph at 34,000ft, the Ar 234 regained for the Luftwaffe much of the immunity from interception they had enjoyed with the Ju 86P and R in the early years of the war.

The first Ar 234 arrived at Juvincourt near Reims in late July, piloted by Leutnant Erich Sommer, who had previously served as a navigator on the Ju 86R. On 2 August 1944 Sommer made history by carrying out the world's first jet PR mission, a ninety-minute flight at 39,000ft covering Allied-held territory around the Cherbourg peninsula, without interference from enemy fighters. More photo-intelligence of the Normandy battle area was said to have been gained in this single flight than the whole of the Luftwaffe's fleet of conventional reconnaissance aircraft had managed in the previous eight weeks.[18]

From then until the end of the war, the Ar 234 served as the Luftwaffe's most important reconnaissance asset, proving almost impossible for even the fastest Allied fighters to shoot down. It was even able to conduct recce runs along the British east coast without interference. To improve survivability still further, a version with rocket motors replacing the two turbojets, the Ar 234R *Höhenaufklärer* (high-altitude scout), was planned. It was anticipated that the 'R' model would reach 54,000ft. None were produced.

Even more ambitious was the DFS 228, another late-war rocket-powered project for conducting reconnaissance at very high altitudes. Drawing on the DFS company's experience of building sailplanes, the 228 was designed by Felix Kracht to meet an RLM requirement issued in 1940. It was intended to be powered by the Walter HWK 509D rocket motor, also fitted to the Me 163 *Komet* interceptor and Bachem Ba 349 *Natter* manned anti-aircraft missile, which it was anticipated would take it up to an astonishing 75,000ft. To overcome the problem of surviving a bale out at such an altitude, the nose-cone housing the pressurised cockpit served as an escape capsule, which in an emergency could be jettisoned from the fuselage. The first prototype, made largely of wood and with a retractable skid undercarriage, was completed in March 1944. As it lacked the rocket motor, unpowered gliding flights were carried out from October. It was also planned to make flights using a Dornier Do 217K as a carrier aircraft, taking the 228 prototype fixed atop the Dornier up to an altitude of 33,000ft before it was launched under the power of its own rocket engine. However, the worsening war situation meant that the Walter motor was never fitted.

A second prototype was completed and joined the test programme at Rechlin in December. It was destroyed in an Allied air raid shortly before the end of the war. The original prototype was captured by US forces at Hörsching in Austria at the beginning of May 1945 and taken back to Britain for analysis, where it's thought to have been scrapped in 1947.

Chapter Seven

Fighters in the Heavens

The immunity from interception enjoyed by the high-flying Ju 86Ps of *Kommando* Rowehl while conducting reconnaissance over southern England during 1940/41 had highlighted a potentially critical weakness in the RAF's defences, a weakness Air Chief Marshal Dowding had recognised even before the Battle got underway, when he had warned of the danger posed by enemy high-altitude bombers (see Chapter Five). Lieutenant General Sir Frederick Pile, C-in-C of Anti-Aircraft Command, shared Dowding's concerns. In a report he submitted in May 1941 to the Cabinet on the future requirements of his Command, he stated:

> It is the considered opinion of the Air Ministry that we may expect by autumn of this year that the enemy will be bombing, both by day and by night, from heights up to at least 40,000ft. Prisoner of War reports confirm the fact that the Germans are producing bombers capable of flying at very great heights. Already there have been attacks in daylight on London from the height of 33,000ft.

In his report, Lieutenant General Pile advised the Cabinet that a more powerful, high velocity anti-aircraft gun, capable of firing a heavier shell than those his Command was currently equipped with, would be required to deal with high-flying enemy intruders. As an all-new AA gun would take some time to enter service, Pile considered that 'the only practical immediate propositions were to use the 5.25" Naval gun, which would enable us to engage targets up to at least 40,000ft, or to take the present 4.5" gun and scale it down to 3.7" giving it an increased charge, and so a higher velocity.'

Of the two options, his preference was for the 5.25-inch Vickers naval gun. 'This gun fires an excellent sized shell up to more than 40,000ft, and is already in production for the Navy,' he explained.[1] The Chiefs of Staff agreed with Pile that 'a heavy AA weapon to deal with targets at very high altitudes was essential' and estimated that around 400 would be required for home defence.[2]

However, it was recognised by the Air Ministry that heavy AA guns could only be a part of the solution. As Dowding had argued in his 1941 despatch, the main defence against the high-altitude bomber could only be provided by the pressurised fighter. In August 1941 several Hurricanes and Spitfires of the AFDU at Duxford were sent to RAF Polebrook in Northamptonshire to take part in fighter affiliation exercises with two of No 90 Squadron's newly acquired American B-17 Flying Fortresses, to develop tactics for intercepting high-flying bombers. Air Marshal Sir Sholto Douglas, Dowding's successor as C-in-C Fighter Command, explained in a post-war report:

Another step taken about this time was the development of a plan for intercepting aircraft capable of flying at very great heights, which it was thought that the Germans might be planning to use against us. After fighters of No. 10 Group had practised making very high-altitude G.C.I. interceptions of Fortresses of Bomber Command, my staff devised a system of control whereby the country was divided into a number of regions each containing an 'area control' connected with a 'central control' designed to co-ordinate their activities. This scheme was to prove useful in 1942 when the Germans sent a number of high-flying Ju 86P reconnaissance [*sic*] aircraft over this country.[3]

Supermarine had already been instructed to develop a pressurised version of the Spitfire, the Mk VI, but its limited endurance would be a serious handicap in high altitude operations, using up most of its fuel in the climb to its maximum ceiling. A larger, twin-engine fighter with greater fuel capacity would be needed.

Anticipating that one day there might be a need for such an aircraft, in October 1939 General Aircraft Limited – which had produced the UK's first pressurised passenger aircraft – submitted a proposal as a private venture to the Air Ministry for a twin-engine, two-seat high-altitude fighter armed with four 20mm cannon, named the GAL.46 (also informally known as the 'Stratosphere Fighter'). At that very early stage in the war, however, the Ministry had little interest in the high-altitude interceptor concept and the company's proposal wasn't pursued. But Dowding's warning about the possible future German use of high-altitude bombers in the summer of 1940 prompted a rethink by the Air Ministry, and in July Specification F.4/40 was issued, which called for a high-performance fighter with heavy cannon armament and a two-man crew housed in a pressurised cockpit, with a ceiling in the region of 45,000ft. Among the companies invited to tender submissions to meet this specification were Fairey, General Aircraft, Hawker and Westland. Fairey was fully committed with other work, while the proposals submitted by Hawker and General Aircraft (which had proposed a slightly revised version of its GAL.46) were quickly ruled out. This left the field open for Westland.

Westland's chief designer W.E.W. 'Teddy' Petter's first submission, the P.13, had a rather unorthodox configuration, with two Merlin engines placed one above and behind the other, driving contra-rotating propellers. This was soon discarded in favour of the more conventional P.14, a large twin-engine machine bearing a strong resemblance to Petter's long-range Whirlwind fighter, which the designer himself described as a 'logical development' of that aircraft. The P.14 was duly selected on 9 January 1941 and, as was standard practice at the time, two prototypes were ordered. Changes requested by the Air Ministry led to the issuing of a revised Specification, F.7/41, in April, the main amendment stipulating that it should now be a single-seater. The ambitious performance targets were also relaxed a little, with a top speed of 415 mph and ceiling of 42,000ft being asked for.

However, the Air Ministry wanted a back-up plan. Westland's Whirlwind project had been beset by development problems – Dowding had correctly predicted that it would present the RAF with 'an infinity of trouble'[4] – and the finished product proved unreliable, failed to meet its performance targets and was cancelled after just 114 had been built, damaging the company's reputation. No doubt fearing the same fate might befall the P.14 project, as an insurance policy the Air Ministry gave the go-ahead for a rival project.

Vickers' 'Tin Mosquito'

The origins of Vickers-Armstrong's contender to meet F.7/41 lay in another, unrelated Specification from 1939 (F.22/39) for a twin-engine fighter with a nose-mounted 40mm cannon. While work on this project proceeded at a relatively leisurely pace, over the next eighteen months the Specification was repeatedly altered, until in spring 1941 Vickers-Armstrong and the Air Ministry agreed to roll the project into the F.7/41 requirement, placing it in direct competition with Westland's P.14.

The Vickers project was designed by a team under Rex Pierson. Their proposal was for a large fighter, featuring an elegant, Spitfire-style elliptical wing and stressed-skin fuselage, which was to be powered by two Merlin 61 engines and carry a very powerful armament of six 20mm cannon in a ventral gunpack. After approving the design, two prototypes were ordered by the Air Ministry on 9 September 1941. The first of these (serial number DZ217) was built at one of Vickers' subsidiary factories, at Foxwarren in Surrey. Given the official designation Type 432 (and, according to some sources, unofficially known as the Mayfly), its all-metal construction and general resemblance to de Havilland's famous multi-purpose warplane led to it being dubbed the 'Tin Mosquito'.[5]

But unlike the 'wooden wonder', the Type 432 would not prove to be a success. Even among the Vickers team, confidence in the project was not high. George Edwards, a senior manager at the company, anticipated that the Type 432 would have a 'troubled life', on account of its complexity. His concerns proved to be well-founded.

DZ217 – lacking a pressurised cockpit – made its maiden flight at RAE Farnborough on Christmas Eve 1942, with test pilot Douglas 'Tommy' Lucke at the controls. The flight, and several more that followed, revealed some serious handling issues, including a tendency for the aircraft to 'snake' while taxiing, and heavy controls. Its performance also fell well short of what the Air Ministry demanded, with a slow rate of climb and maximum speed achieved during the twenty-eight test flights undertaken being 380 mph. Reliability issues with the Merlin 61s when flying above 23,000ft also surfaced. This was the cause of some bewilderment as such problems hadn't been encountered on the Spitfire IX, which used the same powerplant. The Ministry of Aircraft Production ordered that work be halted on the second prototype, which was still under construction, and cancellation of the Type 432 project itself followed in late 1943, the sole prototype being scrapped in 1944.

An unheavenly fighter

Westland, meanwhile, was pressing ahead with work on its P.14, which had been officially christened the 'Welkin', an Old English word for sky or heaven. Like the Vickers Type 432, the Welkin would endure a difficult and protracted gestation. One of the biggest challenges was one common to all pressurised aircraft – mist and frost forming on the cockpit canopy at high altitude. The engineers at Westland overcame this problem by arriving at the same solution as the Junkers' team had with their experimental EF 61 several years earlier, by designing a canopy with a double layer of Perspex, with a constant flow of heated air blown into the space between the two layers.

Power was provided by two Rolls-Royce Merlin 76 engines, with a Rotol compressor attached to the starboard motor driving the pressurisation system. This meant that the physical effects for the pilot of flying at the aircraft's maximum height of 45,000ft was equivalent to that of just 24,000ft. In October 1942 Air Vice Marshal Norman Bottomley, Assistant Chief of the Air Staff (Ops), anticipated that 'early aircraft will have a performance comparable with the Spitfire VII but as engine developments are brought in it will considerably exceed the Spitfire VII in ceiling, which should be approximately 48,000ft'. However, he went on to caution that 'we cannot expect this performance until the end of 1943'.[6]

The first prototype, DG558, was completed at Westland's Yeovil factory in autumn 1942. It was 40ft in length and, for a fighter, had an enormous wingspan of 70ft. Though the prototype was unarmed, production aircraft would be fitted with four 20mm Hispano cannon, with 120 rounds per gun, beneath the forward fuselage. With a fuel capacity of 510 gallons, Westland claimed a range of 1,570 miles for the Welkin.

The first flight was performed at Yeovil by the company's chief test pilot, Harald Penrose, on 1 November 1942. As he had feared, the thick chord wing resulted in serious compressibility issues at high altitude, something he had discussed with Petter but had found the designer reluctant to make changes. The wings also had an alarming tendency to flex in flight. '[The wings] flapped up and down ... like a bird flying!' Penrose recalled in an interview many years later. He also found that 'at certain speeds, in dead-calm air, it made little jerks, like going over cobblestones'. He described this trait as the 'cobblestone motion'.[7] Another complaint was the heat generated in the cockpit by the blower, which left him soaking in sweat. Penrose believed that emerging from the hot cockpit into the cold winter air after test flights was responsible for the bout of near-fatal pneumonia he was struck down with in early 1943.

Even more serious were the engine fires and structural failures that plagued the test aircraft sent to the A & AEE at Boscombe Down for more intensive flight trials. In May 1943 Flight Lieutenant Geoffrey Brunner was on a high-altitude test flight in DG558 when it suffered an engine fire, as described in the citation for the Bar to his AFC he was awarded for his actions during this flight:

> one of the engines commenced to emit large quantities of smoke and oil. A course was set for base, but smoke started to enter the cockpit, and the aircraft entered a steep dive. Efforts to rectify this were at first unavailing but eventually partial control was regained after much height had been lost and Flight Lieutenant Brunner succeeded in reaching an airfield, lowered his undercarriage and landed successfully. Through his skill and courage, a valuable aircraft was saved

from complete destruction and this enabled the cause of the failure to be ascertained. The high skill and gallantry displayed by the pilot on this occasion was most commendable and set an outstanding example of coolness, efficiency and devotion to duty.[8]

Fellow test pilot Philip Lucas had a similar experience while flying the Welkin at Boscombe Down. He had been in the air for fifteen minutes and was still climbing when he looked over and saw 'the whole port wing on fire'. He was instructed by ground control to land at an emergency airstrip. His difficulties then increased when the aircraft's hydraulics packed up. 'So I was in a very bad place – having to land this thing without brakes, no flaps, and on a [runway] I'd never used before,' he recalled.[9] Nevertheless, Lucas managed to land safely and escape from the burning aircraft. Moments later, the blazing port wing fell off.

After several more crashes and forced landings during the latter part of 1943, most the result of engine fires, flight trials of the Welkin at high altitude were temporarily suspended until the engine problems could be resolved.

On a more positive note, the cockpit arrangement and absence of misting on the canopy at altitude earned praise from the test pilots. 'With high-altitude aircraft you have trouble with cockpit icing up and misting at high-altitude. This never happened on the Welkin … I never had any high-altitude visibility problems with it,' revealed Eric 'Winkle' Brown, one of those who test flew the aircraft. However, while Brown felt that 'from an engineering point of view, it was interesting,' his overall opinion was that the Welkin was 'not an outstanding aeroplane'.[10]

By 1944, with the high-altitude threat to the UK greatly diminished, it was proposed to re-equip No 1 and 165 Squadron with the Welkin and assign them to the Allied Expeditionary Air Force, in preparation for the invasion of France in the summer. But this idea met with a cool response from Air Commodore Wilfred Freebody, Senior Technical Officer with the AEAF, who wrote on 16 February 1944:

> I think it would be fair comment to say that no-one is at present enthusiastic in their reception of this aircraft into service. In meeting design requirements for high altitude work the firm have produced a highly specialised type which cannot easily be adapted to any other use. Furthermore, the Welkin has been so slow in its development that standard types of day and night fighters have surpassed it in performance and, with a few minor qualifications, shown themselves capable of undertaking the work for which the Welkin was designed.

Freebody also predicted that there would be many teething troubles with the type and that it would be much harder to maintain in the field than the Spitfire VII. 'Since the aircraft is twin-engined and large (70ft span) the number of maintenance personnel required to look after it will be much greater than are required for a Spitfire VII squadron.' The Welkin's poor manoeuvrability revealed during flight testing also suggested it would fare badly in a dogfight with German fighters. 'The prototype and early production aircraft have a history of aileron trouble and it has been difficult to obtain a reasonable degree of manoeuvrability without incurring aileron over-balance,' Freebody pointed out. 'Whatever may be the outcome of the aileron development story, it seems highly desirable that this aircraft should not be forced to engage in combat with single-engined fighters of equivalent performance.'

Air Commodore Freebody's assessment of the Welkin concluded:

> My personal view is that the single-seater Welkin can only be regarded as a weapon for defence against sub-stratosphere bombing attacks, and it is for the Air Staff to decide, with the knowledge of any potential threat of such attack which may exist, whether a requirement for the Welkin now holds. In making this decision it should be borne in mind that the Welkin in many respects, including performance, is inferior to other types using the same engine or engines … As far as the immediate operations of A.E.A.F. units are concerned, I consider that the effort which we shall need to put forth in bringing the Welkin into service is not worth the meagre return that this effort will give us.[11]

Two examples, painted in the same light blue colour scheme as used on the RAF's PR Spitfires, were assigned to the Fighter Interception Unit at RAF Wittering in Cambridgeshire from May 1944, where they were used in exercises to refine tactics and gain further experience in high-altitude interception.

Efforts were also made during this time to improve the Welkin's performance by installing a liquid oxygen injection system then under development, which it was hoped would raise its absolute ceiling to 47,000ft. But technical problems with the system continually delayed flight trials.

By winter 1944 the Air Staff had come to the view that, as far as the air defence of Great Britain was concerned, current and new fighter types, like the jet-powered Gloster Meteor, could perform the task just as effectively. On 17 December 1944, Air Commodore George Lawson, Director of Operations (Air Defence), wrote:

> From the air defence point of view, on the existing performance of the aircraft the facts are that it is inferior in performance to our best day and night fighters below 40,000ft. With the introduction of the jet fighter with its superior high altitude performance the production of the Welkin for day interception is no longer necessary.[12]

The multiple issues with the Welkin revealed during testing, combined with the diminishing threat of enemy attack from extreme altitude, led the Air Ministry to cancel a second order for 200 Welkins. Of the initial contract for 100 Mk Is, seventy-seven (including the two prototypes) were completed by Westland, while a further twenty-six airframes were built without engines.

With dozens of aircraft having already rolled off the Westland production line, throughout 1944 the RAF's Technical Requirements section considered and rejected several alternative roles for the unwanted stratospheric interceptor, including fighter–bomber ('For this role the lower altitude performance was quite unacceptable'); photo–reconnaissance ('Inadequate view from the pressure cabin at high altitude'); meteorological duties ('Aircraft could not carry the necessary equipment to make it worthwhile for this role'); and high-speed target tug ('Inadequate performance when towing the target').[13]

The only alternative employment deemed suitable for the Welkin was as a radar-equipped night-fighter, though this would require substantial modification of the airframe. But Air Commodore Freebody also expressed doubts about this proposal, believing that the aircraft would offer little benefit over the latest version of the Mosquito in service with ADGB:

> As a general purpose night-fighter it will compare unfavourably with the Mosquito. It might, however, be the only means of meeting very high altitude enemy aircraft equipped for jamming our radar apparatus, both ground and airborne. It will, however, be a long time before we see this two-seater in production and, in terms of the war against Germany, it is doubtful if the Welkin will be available by the time when it would be opportune or possible for the enemy to make such attacks.[14]

Nevertheless, a prototype was ordered, to be converted from a Welkin Mk I (DX836), with plans to convert sixty more Mk Is if all went well. The resultant Welkin NF.Mk II was distinguished by its bulbous nose containing the A.I. Mk VIII radar and an enlarged cockpit, accommodating an observer/radar operator, who was seated behind the pilot, facing aft. The sole NF.Mk II built, given the serial number PF370, made its first flight on 23 October 1944. The additional weight of the radar and second crewman meant that the top speed and ceiling were a little lower than the Mk I day fighter, at 370 mph and 42,500ft.

With the air threat to the UK from the Luftwaffe negligible by that time, however, Air Commodore Lawson decided that 'there is no immediate requirement for a very high altitude night fighter' and production plans for the NF.Mk II were shelved.[15]

Debate then turned to what to do with the sizeable number of completed Welkins for which the RAF now had no practical use. 'I feel that we should make some effort to get a decision on the future of the Welkin at an early date,' wrote Lawson's deputy in a minute of 19 February 1945, entitled 'Future of the Welkin'. 'I have no doubt a considerable amount of money has been put into the project and if the aircraft is not to be of any use to us the sooner we cut our loss the better.'[16]

No immediate decision was reached, but as the war in Europe approached its conclusion the Ministry of Aircraft Production was becoming impatient to finally resolve the fate of the Westland Welkin, if only to free up space. 'M.A.P. are concerned about the storage of these aircraft which are very liable to corrosion and require considerable maintenance if they are to be kept in a serviceable condition. Moreover, they are not suitable for storage in the open, and absorb considerable hangar space,' Wing Commander Cheatle wrote to the Director of Policy (Air), Group Captain Douglas Macfadyen, on 26 April

1945. 'We are, as you are aware, doing our utmost to reduce all redundant stocks of unwanted aircraft, and the Welkin, for which no operational or training use has been discovered, seems to be an obvious choice for addition to the list of obsolete types scheduled for breakdown.'

It wasn't until two days after VE Day that the decision was finally made to scrap the Welkin, with only a few examples escaping the smelter, to be used for research purposes for a short period. 'The C.A.S. has agreed that there is no RAF requirement for the Welkin and that a small number only should be retained for research ... All surplus Welkins should be reduced to produce,' advised Macfadyen.[17]

The sole Welkin NF.Mk II night-fighter prototype was retained as a radar testbed after the war before also being scrapped in the late 1940s.

Yankee high-flyers

On the other side of the Atlantic, the United States was also developing prototype high-altitude fighters with pressurised cockpits, though none of their various projects would reach production status.

A single example of the Lockheed P-38 Lightning was modified with a pressurised cockpit early in the war, for experimental purposes. Designated the XP-38A, it carried out evaluation flights in late 1942 but remained a one-off. A more radical re-engineering of the P-38 by Lockheed was the XP-49. Looking almost identical to the Lightning, and sharing many of the same parts, the main difference with the standard P-38

Captain Rudolph 'Shorty' Schroeder, an early pioneer of high-altitude aviation, beside the Bristol Fighter in which he set a world altitude record of 28,900 ft on 18 September 1918. (US Air Force National Museum)

Above: Incorporating a fully pressurized cabin, the experimental Ju 49 helped establish the Junkers company as a world leader in the field of stratospheric flight. (Courtesy of Charlotte Junkers)

Left: This shot of the interior of the Ju 49's revolutionary pressure cabin illustrates the confined space and how limited the view was out of the porthole windows. (Courtesy of Charlotte Junkers)

The British equivalent of the Ju 49 was the Bristol Type 138A. Though lacking a pressure cabin, this research aircraft set several altitude records in the late 1930s. (© Crown Copyright)

Entering Luftwaffe service in 1936, the Junkers Ju 86 proved a disappointment as a bomber but received a new lease of life when a small number were heavily modified to serve as extreme altitude reconnaissance aircraft. (Public domain)

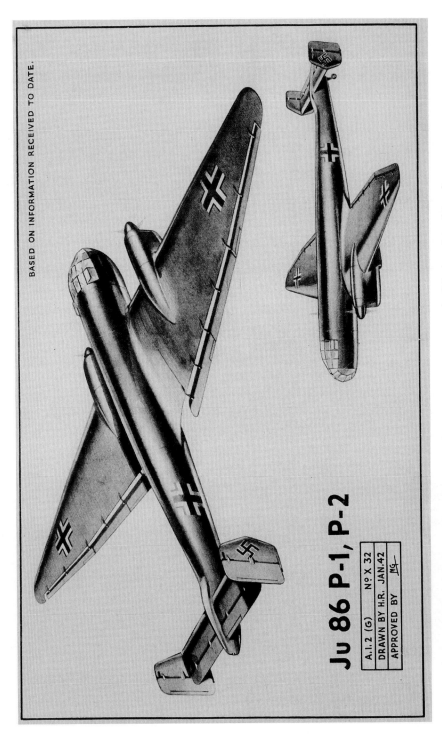

Ju 86 P-1, P-2

A.I.2 (G)	Nº X 32
DRAWN BY H.R.	JAN.42
APPROVED BY	MG

A British illustration from 1942 of the Junkers Ju 86P reconnaissance aircraft. (National Archives)

The real thing. Capable of reaching 42,000 ft and almost impossible to shoot down, the Ju 86P was a cause of considerable concern to the RAF during the early war years. (Courtesy of Chris Goss)

The Junkers Jumo 207 inline diesel engine, which powered the Ju 86P, allowed these aircraft to attain their then unprecedented operating altitude. (Courtesy of National Air and Space Museum)

Gun camera footage from a specially lightened Spitfire Mk V of 103 Maintenance Unit of an attack on a Ju 86R – an improved version of the 'P' model – over Egypt in 1942. Though damaged, on this occasion the Ju 86R escaped. (National Archives)

Following the flawed Mk VI, the Spitfire Mk VII was a far more successful attempt at adapting the legendary fighter for extreme altitude operations. Like the Mk VI, it was instantly recognisable by its distinctive pointed wingtips. (US National Archives and Records Administration)

The PR.Mk XIX was the ultimate high-altitude reconnaissance version of the Spitfire. This example, PS915 (known as 'The Last') still flies today with the Battle of Britain Memorial Flight. (© Crown Copyright)

The Dornier Do 217P, which reached over 49,000 ft in test flights, was a leading contender to replace the Ju 86R in the reconnaissance role but ultimately never entered full production. (Public domain)

The failure to introduce a suitable replacement for the Ju 86P and R series in the mid-War period forced the Luftwaffe to rely on recce versions of the Messerschmitt Bf 109G to fulfil their PR needs. This is an example of the long-range G-6 R3 variant. (Courtesy of National Air and Space Museum)

Dubbed the 'Tin Mosquito', the Type 432 was Vickers' attempt to meet the Air Ministry's requirement for a stratospheric, pressurized fighter to defend Britain from an expected high-altitude Luftwaffe bombing offensive. (© BAE SYSTEMS)

The Type 432's main competitor to fill the high-altitude interceptor role was the Westland Welkin. Though capable of reaching 45,000 ft, the Welkin's development was plagued with problems and none of the 100 examples manufactured entered squadron service. (National Archives)

The Americans also developed a range of high-altitude fighters, such as the Republic XP-47J 'Superbolt', a pressurized variant of the P-47 Thunderbolt. (US Air Force)

McDonnell Aircraft's response to the USAAF's request for a pressurized fighter was the XP-67 'Moonbat', which failed to progress beyond the prototype stage. (US Air Force)

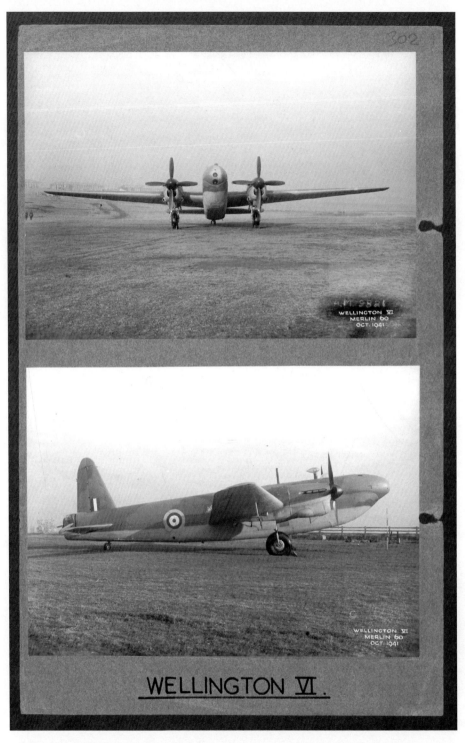

WELLINGTON VI.

The Wellington Mk VI was a heavily modified, high-altitude variant of Vickers' dependable bomber. This is the Mk VI prototype. (National Archives)

Intended as a successor to the outstanding Avro Lancaster, the Vickers Windsor was designed from the outset to be capable of bombing from 45,000 ft. (© BAE SYSTEMS)

Based on the highly successful B-25 Mitchell, the North American XB-28 'Dragon' was one of several pressurized bomber projects developed for the USAAF. (US Air Force)

With a high ceiling and impressive performance, the Mitsubishi Ki-46 provided the Japanese with an excellent reconnaissance platform in the early part of the Pacific War, until the arrival of improved Allied fighters caused losses to mount. This Ki-46 was destroyed on Iwo Jima in February 1945. (Courtesy of Naval History and Heritage Command)

Boeing B-29 Superfortresses of 21st Bomber Command dropping incendiaries on Yokohama on 29 May 1945. The relatively high ceiling of this American giant presented a formidable challenge to Japan's air defences. (Courtesy of US Air Force National Museum)

Seen here in USAAF markings after the Japanese surrender, the Nakajima G8N1 *Renzan* was one of several ambitious, pressurized bomber projects developed by the Japanese during the war to strike back at the Continental United States. (Public domain)

Ever improving British air defences as the war progressed led to Germany developing bombers intended to rely on their altitude to avoid fighter interception, like the Henschel Hs 130. (Public domain)

Developed in reconnaissance, night-fighter and bomber variants, the Junkers Ju 388 was capable of reaching 43,000 ft, though only a very few of the 'L' reconnaissance version are believed to have reached frontline units before the German surrender. This Ju 388 is seen in US hands after its capture in May 1945. (Courtesy of Chris Goss)

The quest for altitude did not end in 1945. Capable of reaching 85,000 ft, Lockheed's extraordinary SR-71 'Blackbird' was the Cold War equivalent of stratospheric spy planes like the Ju 86P. (US Air Force National Museum)

was the replacement of the Allison V-1710 engines with turbo-supercharged Continental XI-1430 units. The XP-49 made its first flight on 14 November 1942, with Lockheed test pilot Joseph C. Towle at the controls. Six weeks later the testing programme was suspended after Towle had to make a forced landing when the aircraft suffered electrical and hydraulic failure. Testing resumed after repairs had been completed in February 1943, with the USAAF taking delivery of the only prototype in June at Muroc Airfield for further evaluation. But the Air Force judged that the XP-49 offered no real advantage in performance over the latest versions of the P-38 and so the project was shelved later that year.

Republic Aviation's response to a USAAC specification issued in February 1940 for a high-speed, high-altitude fighter was the XP-69, which was given the in-house company designation AP-18. Two prototypes were ordered in December 1941, though construction of the first of these didn't begin until almost a year later. The XP-69 was dropped in May 1943 before a prototype was completed, as Republic focused its attention on another high-altitude fighter project, the XP-72, which seemed to offer greater promise.

With a Pratt & Whitney R-4360 Wasp Major engine, the XP-72 was expected to have a ceiling of around 42,000ft. In the wake of the XP-69's cancellation, two prototypes were ordered, with the first flight taking place in February 1944, from Republic Field in Farmingdale, New York. The testing phase went relatively smoothly and a contract for 100 aircraft was placed in late 1944, only to be rescinded shortly afterwards as USAAF interest shifted towards jet-powered fighter development.

In November 1942 Republic also proposed to the USAAF a lightened version of its heavyweight P-47 Thunderbolt fighter to improve its high-altitude performance. Designated the XP-47J (and also referred to as the 'Superbolt'), two prototypes were ordered. Weight-saving measures included reducing the armament from eight to six .50 calibre machine-guns and removing a fuel tank aft of the cockpit, while the addition of a CH-5 supercharger to the R-2800 engine necessitated a redesign of the cowling. Only one prototype was completed, this aircraft featuring the 'razorback' canopy of the earlier Thunderbolt models rather than the later bubble canopy. Test flights began in November 1943 and showed that the XP-47J had excellent performance, setting a world speed record in level flight for a propeller-driven aircraft of 505 mph in August 1944. But, like the XP-72, it came along too late in the war to justify being put into production.

To meet a 1940 request to provide the USAAC with a very long-range fighter and bomber destroyer, capable of operating at high altitude, the Curtiss-Wright aircraft company proposed the XP-71, which would've been the largest fighter of the Second World War. Curtiss' design featured an unusual twin-engine configuration driven by a contra-rotating 'pusher' propeller, and was planned to incorporate a very heavy armament of one 75mm and two 37mm cannon in the nose. With a pressurised cockpit, it would have been capable of reaching 40,000ft. Impressed by the design, the USAAC ordered the customary two prototypes. A mock-up was completed in November 1942 but Curtiss' other commitments and the dwindling enemy bomber threat by the mid-war years led to the cancellation of the XP-71 in October 1943 before a prototype could be built.

McDonnell Aircraft also attempted to fulfil the long-range, high-altitude interceptor requirement. Their submission, the XP-67 (unofficially called the 'Moonbat'), was another large, twin-engine machine, intended to carry heavy firepower. The prototype began flight testing in January 1944, but the Continental XIV-1430 V-12 engines proved to be both underpowered and prone to catching fire. The destruction of the only prototype in a forced landing on 6 September 1944 dealt a fatal blow to the programme and the XP-67 was officially axed a few days later.

Chapter Eight

Stratospheric *Störangriff*

T he inability of Bomber Command to destroy German military and industrial targets by night, highlighted in the Butt Report of August 1941, led to the issuing of the controversial 'Area Bombing Directive' in February 1942. This instructed Bomber Command 'To focus attacks on the morale of the enemy civil population and in particular the industrial workers', paving the way for indiscriminate mass raids on Germany's cities.[1]

First to feel the effects of Bomber Command's new strategy was the city of Lubeck. On the night of 28/29 March 1942, a force of 234 Stirlings, Wellingtons, Hampdens and Manchesters bombed the port city, killing over 300 people, injuring almost a thousand more and destroying around 4,000 buildings. As Nazi propaganda minister Josef Goebbels wrote in his diary after the raid: 'No German city has ever before been attacked so severely from the air.'[2]

Infuriated, Hitler demanded intensified bombing of Britain in reprisal. On 14 April 1942 the Luftwaffe's operations headquarters received the following signal:

> The Führer has ordered that the air war against England
> is to be given a more aggressive stamp. Accordingly,
> when targets are being selected, preference is to be

given to those where attacks are likely to have the greatest possible effect on civilian life. Besides raids on ports and industry, terror attacks of a retaliatory nature are to be carried out against towns other than London.[3]

This led to the so-called 'Baedeker Raids', after the tourist guidebook used to select targets, based on their historic and cultural, rather than military, significance. Among the towns bombed between 23 April and 6 June 1942 were Exeter, Bath, Canterbury, Norwich and York, killing over 1,600 civilians.

As RAF raids on Germany became steadily more destructive under the direction of Bomber Command's new C-in-C, Air Chief Marshal Arthur Harris, including with the first 'Thousand Bomber Raid' on Cologne in May 1942, the Luftwaffe also commenced *störangriff* (nuisance raids) against England. These were small scale 'tip-and-run' attacks carried out by Bf 109 and Fw 190 *Jabos*. Flying fast and very low, below radar coverage, they proved particularly difficult for Fighter Command to counter.

While the 'tip and run' raiders were harassing the British at low level, Goering ordered that these should be supplemented with attacks made at very high altitude in daylight, above the ceiling of the defending RAF fighters. These attacks would be carried out by the Ju 86R-2.

The R-2 was a converted bomber variant of the improved Ju 86R-1 photo-reconnaissance aircraft, which had entered service in early 1942. It differed from the reconnaissance version only in being equipped with the Lofte 7 bombsight and having the camera installation removed along with the defensive armament and armour plating, to compensate for the additional weight of the bombload, which amounted to a single 551lb bomb. Four aircraft (serial numbers T5+PM, T5+QM, T5+RM and T9+PM) were converted to the R-2 standard and arrived at Oranienburg in the summer, with a total of four crewmen: Leutnant Erich Sommer, Feldwebel Horst Goetz, Unteroffizier Gerd Albrecht and Flieger Hauptingenieur Werner Altrogge, who had flown recce missions in the earlier Ju 86P model over England and the Soviet Union in 1940/41. Trial bomb runs were carried out at a height of 42,500ft at the Rechlin test centre, conducted by Sommer and Goetz. Unfortunately, several French PoWs working in the fields where the bomb was dropped had not been cleared from the area beforehand and received minor shrapnel injuries from the blast. Despite this, Sommer regarded the test a success. 'Everything had worked satisfactorily. The fuse performed properly. The ride in the pressurised cockpit was agreeable with us being able to sit there in our normal uniforms, without oxygen masks. Even the noise level was quite low.'[4]

Höhenkampf Kommando

Leutnant Sommer was appointed commander of the small unit, which was given the title *Höhenkampf Kommando* (High-Altitude Detachment). Despatched to the Luftwaffe air base at Beauvais, forty miles north of Paris, the unit was assigned to the operational command of KG 6. However, their arrival coincided with the Allies ill-fated landings at Dieppe on 19 August. With the Beauvais base being heavily used by German fighters to help repel the landings, the Ju 86R-2s were forced to immediately decamp to Orly. The successful repulse of the Allied landings allowed the unit to return to Beauvais on 20 August. Due to a shortage of crews trained on the type, however, a maximum of two of the four aircraft that made up the *Höhenkampf Kommando* could be sent out at one time on a raid. Meanwhile, Goering's ignorance of the practical limitations of achieving any degree of accuracy with bombing at altitudes of over 42,000ft was revealed when he sent the unit a telex, ordering that they should concentrate on attacking railway targets. Sommer said that they 'contemptuously put the telex aside and ignored it'.[5]

The British had been aware for some time that the Germans had developed a bomber version of their successful Ju 86P/R series reconnaissance aircraft and had accumulated quite a lot of information on the type – they just didn't know when they would be used. An RAF Air Intelligence report, dated 22 December 1941 and entitled 'German Stratosphere Bombers', stated:

Information has been received from a reliable source giving details of new Junkers high-altitude bombers.

Ju 86 P-1 (bomber):

This is a version of the Ju 86 developed for high-altitudes with sealed pressure-cabin and Jumo 207 A/1 diesel engines. The maximum bombload is 2,200lbs and the operational ceiling up to 39,300ft with this load. The speed given, which can be maintained at heights over

20,000ft, is 186 mph and the fuel tankage of 475 gallons
will give 6½ hours endurance. The crew is given as 2,
and no armament is fitted.[6]

Though overestimating the maximum bombload that could be
carried by the aircraft, this report was otherwise fairly accurate.

The high-altitude bombing campaign so long feared by the
British finally opened on the afternoon of 24 August 1942,
when Sommer and Goetz – both of whom had previously
flown bombing missions against England with KG 100 – took
off from Beauvais in T9+PM. They were plotted by British
radar crossing the English coast at Selsey Bill at 1448 hrs.
Sommer and Goetz's target was the garrison town of Aldershot,
but instead they mistakenly dropped their single bomb over
Camberley, six miles away. Fifteen Spitfire Vbs were scrambled
in response to what Fighter Command reported as an enemy
aircraft flying over southern England 'at abnormally high
altitude'. Three sections made visual contact with the Ju 86R-2
as it turned back for France, but none were able to intercept.

One section saw its vapour trail climb from 29,000ft to
an estimated height of 38,000ft and followed it across
the Channel, but could not climb up to it. Another
section sighted the aircraft at 38,000ft when themselves
at 36,000ft, but could not climb up to it. One pilot of
the third section blacked out briefly when climbing
towards the aircraft and returned to base. The other
pilots of this section climbed towards it from 33,000ft,

but could not reach it. This pilot also estimates its height at 38,000ft.[7]

Sommer and Goetz landed back safely at Beauvais at 1722 hrs.

Meanwhile, the second Ju 86R-2, crewed by Altrogge and Albrecht, crossed the coast at the Isle of Wight and dropped its bomb on Southampton at 1541 hrs, causing a single fatality, a 50-year-old woman. Again, several Spitfires were scrambled to intercept, but again the Junkers easily outclimbed them. 'One section of Spitfire VB sighted this aircraft at 32,000ft when themselves at 25,000ft. They climbed to 37,000ft but the enemy aircraft still climbed away from them,' revealed an RAF Air Intelligence report.[8] This second Ju 86R-2 left the country over Sussex just before 1600 hrs.

There was some confusion as to what type of bomber had been used on the day's raids, most of the Spitfire pilots who made visual contact misidentifying the high-flying intruders as Dornier Do 217s, although Air Intelligence thought it 'highly improbable that even a specially developed Do 217 could attain a height of 38,000ft'. On being presented with comparative silhouettes of the Do 217 and Ju 86R, the pilots 'withdrew their previous identification and identified the aircraft as a Ju 86'.[9]

The next day Sommer and Goetz were back, their Ju 86R-2 being picked up as it headed over the Channel at 34,000ft. The Germans flew over the Isle of Wight, Southampton, Swindon, and the outskirts of London, their plan being to trigger air raid alerts across as wide an area as possible and thus cause maximum disruption to industry. But the crew were unaware that the British Government had ordered local authorities to regard single intruders by day as harmless reconnaissance flights and so the air raid sirens were not sounded. The RAF, however, did react, sending up nine Spitfires, though none come close to the Ju 86R-2's altitude. 'We watched as interested spectators while these zig-zagged thousands of feet below with their exhausts smoking in an attempt to gain altitude,' Sommer later wrote. 'There was much chatter on their radios which gave our listening post, at Meldekopf Birk near Cherbourg, the opportunity to locate British units and plot the frequency ranges which they were using.'[10] They dropped their bomb on Stanstead St Margarets in Hertfordshire at 1655 hrs (the crew believed they had attacked Luton) before flying back to France unmolested.

Within hours Goebbels' propaganda ministry gleefully announced on German state radio that the *Höhenkampf Kommando* had carried out its first successful daylight raids on England, though of course omitting the fact that the raiding force comprised only two bombers.

The raids so far had caused little damage and few casualties. But that was all to change on the morning of 28 August, when Sommer and Goetz raided Bristol. At 0912 hrs a pair of Spitfire Vbs of No 310 (Czech) Sqn spotted their Ju 86R at high altitude near Portland but were unable to engage it. A pair of twin-engine Westland Whirlwinds of No 263 Sqn were also scrambled from RAF Colerne, which 'struggled to 24,000 but saw nothing'.[11]

In clear blue skies, over Broad Weir in Bristol's city centre, the Germans released their bomb, which landed among the morning rush-hour traffic. With no warning of the impending attack due to the decision not to sound the air raid sirens, the shock and devastation caused by the 551lb bomb in the busy street was enormous. One woman who was blown off her feet by the blast said that it 'came like a bolt from the blue'.[12] Three crowded buses were engulfed in flames from the explosion, with many passengers trapped inside. Margaret Lowry, a passenger in one of the buses, described the moment the bomb exploded:

> I was looking out of the window when there was this almighty flash. We didn't hear the bomb because it was too close. Then the blast came, but the bus went on. I was told later that the driver had been killed instantly and that his foot was still on the pedal.[13]

As the Ju 86R departed it was fired on by AA guns, but none of the shells exploded above 30,000ft. In total, forty-seven people were killed in the attack and a further fifty injured, half of them seriously. Those killed ranged from a baby to a 74-year-old.

The *Höhenkampf Kommando* kept up the pressure. In the afternoon, Altrogge and Albrecht attacked Cardiff, their bomb hitting the city's Roath district, killing two and injuring several others. On 29 August the target was Swindon, this early morning raid by Sommer and Goetz killing eight people and seriously injuring six more. While making their escape, two Spitfire IXs of No 401 (Canadian) Sqn were alerted to the presence of the high-flying intruder near Horsham and gave chase, as a Fighter Command intelligence report explained:

> One Spitfire saw an E/A at 32,000ft when our a/c was 1,000ft below. The Spitfire followed and tried to get up

sun. When the Spitfire was at 39,000ft the E/A was still 700ft above. Both Spitfire and E/A continued to climb and Spitfire reached his maximum height of 40,000ft climbing at 86 mph I.A.S. The E/A reached 41,500ft and appeared to be labouring as if he had also reached maximum height, and Spitfire had to break away owing to oxygen running short. The second Spitfire broke away at 30,000ft.[14]

Nor did the pressurised Spitfire VIs enjoy any more luck when another Ju 86R-2, flown by Albrecht and Altrogge, carried out the second raid of the day, hitting Cambridge in the early afternoon. After spotting the bomber's vapour trails high above their position, two Mk VIs of No 124 Sqn flying from RAF Debden climbed to 37,000ft. However, 'the e/a apparently sighted the Spitfires and drew away with ease, still climbing'. Low on fuel, the Spitfire pilots were forced to abandon the chase over North Foreland.[15]

On 30 August it was the turn of Chelmsford to be visited by the Ju 86R-2, Sommer and Goetz flying T5+RM on this occasion. The bomb hit a warehouse but failed to explode. Engine trouble forced the second Ju 86R crew to abandon their sortie of the day an hour and a half into the flight and return to Beauvais.

The Luftwaffe's high-altitude bombing offensive was by now causing serious concern at the highest levels of Government. The subject was raised at a Cabinet meeting chaired by Churchill on 31 August 1942, where it was agreed that casualties suffered in future high-altitude raids should be publicly downplayed, so as not to embolden the Germans. Minutes of the meeting stated:

> The Home Secretary and Minister of Home Security said that on Friday, Saturday and Sunday there had been daylight raids on Bristol, Swindon and Chelmsford by high-flying aircraft. In the raid on Bristol 41 people had been killed [*sic*] and 28 seriously injured, two buses having been gutted, with passengers trapped inside.

> In discussion, it was stated that, although no figures of casualties had been quoted, the publication in the Press of the fact that two buses had been destroyed and passengers trapped inside must have given the enemy a fairly good idea of the success achieved by this isolated raider. This could be avoided, e.g. by summarising the results of several raids in one communique.[16]

After a brief lull, the attacks resumed on 4 September, when Ramsgate was targeted. This time two Spitfire IXs of No 133 (Eagle) Squadron at Biggin Hill were sent aloft, catching up with the Ju 86R flying over North Foreland at 40,000ft. One of the pilots, Pilot Officer Beaty, fired a burst from his cannon and machine guns from below, and reported that he hit the underside of the aircraft. Beaty's engine then began smoking and cut out, forcing the American to bale out at 20,000ft, where he landed fifteen miles east of Manston, suffering minor injuries. The Ju 86R, which in fact hadn't been hit, returned safely to Beauvais. A section of Mk VIs from No 124 Sqn was also sent up after the Ju 86R, also to no avail. 'These Huns are certainly persistent,' commented the Squadron ORB after the raid.[17]

The next day Luton was attacked, Sommer and Goetz flying a winding route that took them over Portsmouth, Oxford, Bicester and Hatfield before releasing their bomb, which killed four people. Flight Lieutenant Emil Foit and Sergeant Karel Pernica of No 310 (Czech) Sqn at RAF Warmwell were scrambled in their Spitfire Vbs, sighting the Junkers fifteen miles north of London at 40,000ft and misidentifying it as an Fw 200 Condor. 'Blue Section followed and attempted to climb to e/a level, but only managed to reach some 37,000ft and could gain no further height.' The two Czechs eventually had to give up the chase as the Ju 86R-2 crossed the coast at Brighton. 'This encounter is interesting,' noted the Squadron's ORB, 'as it shows that the Hun has large aircraft that can get up higher than our Spitfires do.'[18] Typhoons of No 609 and Spitfires of No 302 Squadron also attempted to intercept during this raid, but were similarly unsuccessful.

In the afternoon Altrogge and Albrecht set off to bomb Brighton, but again engine problems forced them to abandon the mission without dropping their bomb. Altrogge and Albrecht's run of misfortune continued on the 6th, when a sortie to bomb Aldershot in the afternoon had to be abandoned mid-flight, again due to the Ju 86R's temperamental diesel powerplants. Sommer and Goetz, however, successfully completed their mission, an attack on Gloucester, though they were chased by a pair of stripped-down Spitfire Vbs of No 501 Squadron, one of the fighters getting to within 1,500ft of the bomber's altitude of 42,000ft before engine trouble forced the pilot to break off.

A P-38 Lightning of the USAAF's 94th Fighter Squadron, newly arrived in England, was also scrambled. When at 38,000ft, First Lieutenant Lewis Murdock put his P-38's nose up and fired a short burst but failed to hit the raider.

The Spitfire Mk VIs had another attempt at reaching the Ju 86R on 9 September, when Pilot Officer Blanchard and Sergeant Goodyear of No 616 Sqn took off from RAF Great Sampford at 1530 hrs and caught up with the enemy raider flying south of Clacton at 38,000ft. The Squadron ORB reported: 'Still climbing and keeping the e/a in sight, they were eventually ordered by the controller to jettison their machine gun ammunition and finally reached 38,100ft and 38,500ft respectively over Ramsgate. The Hun was then at from 41/42,000ft.' Unable to climb any further, Blanchard and Goodyear were forced to break off and return to base.[19]

At a Cabinet meeting on 7 September, the subject of enemy high-altitude bombing of the UK was again raised and the problems of intercepting the Ju 86R with the Spitfire models currently equipping the RAF's air defence squadrons were discussed. 'Spitfire VI won't make the height [of the Ju 86R],' it was noted. The Spitfire Mk IX, on the other hand, 'will do the height, but no pressure cabin'.[20]

The question of how to combat the high-altitude raids was also now being examined with urgency by senior RAF officers, including the Chief of the Air Staff, Air Chief Marshal Sir Charles Portal. Among the options put forward were to accelerate delivery of the Spitfire Mk VII, speed up development of the Welkin, or 'raise the development of a pressurised suit for pilots to a high priority. This for possible use in Spitfire

IXs.' Of these, Portal favoured the first option, pointing out that 'it seems that the Spitfire VII will be almost as good as the Welkin except for its lack of surface which may be got over by development in tactics'. The deployment of even just a few of these fighters, he felt, 'may result in such a high percentage of success against these high flyers by day that the enemy will cease to use them'.

Production of the Mk VII was running behind schedule, however, with the Controller General's Department of the MAP stating that the type wouldn't be ready for operations until later that year, with a total of only four examples due to be produced in October and November, rising to five in December and then ten by January. 'One of the causes for this very disappointing output,' noted the MAP's Controller of Research and Development, 'is the Air Ministry decision in June to reverse the existing priorities in favour of the Spitfire VIII.'

As for the Welkin, the first production example wasn't expected to be ready until May 1943, with an average of just two or three rolling off the production lines each month for the rest of the year. With Westland also committed to producing Supermarine Seafires – the navalised variant of the Spitfire – for the Royal Navy, the CRD observed that 'any acceleration [of the Welkin programme] must therefore be at the expense of the Admiralty requirements'. While the Assistant Chief of the Air Staff (Technical), Air Vice Marshal Ralph Sorley, thought it 'highly desirable to try and bring forward the Welkin', Portal ruled this out, responding that, 'The Prime Minister has given super-priority to modern fighters for aircraft carriers.' The CAS also impressed upon his subordinates the importance of keeping the situation in proportion. While 'it is of course necessary to develop the means of dealing with the high altitude bomber,' he wrote in a minute of 17 September, 'it would be wrong to lose our sense of perspective and to rush into action which may seriously affect other and even more important requirements'.[21]

Air Vice Marshal Norman Bottomley, Assistant Chief of the Air Staff (Ops), was pessimistic about the prospects of getting either of these high-altitude interceptors into frontline service in the immediate future. 'The situation is not favourable to us,' he wrote gloomily on 16 September, although he hoped that there might be 'an improvement in the situation by December and possibly a reasonably satisfactory state of affairs by March 1943'.[22]

This left the pressure suit, a new version of which was then under development for the RAF. Bottomley explained that 'the pressurised suit, if it can be made effective, will enable normal high performance fighters to be used effectively at high altitudes. Furthermore, it would appear that accelerating the development of these pressurised suits will not have any repercussions in other directions.' But the CRD was sceptical, commenting that he had 'little hope of anything useful coming out of the use of pressure suits in an aircraft such as the Spitfire IX'. Sorley was concerned about the length of time it would take to bring the suits into operation, stating that it was 'not expected to be complete for another month' and adding:

Assuming that it was found suitable for a pilot flying a Spitfire IX, which from C.R.D.'s remarks is not considered likely, we should then have to have made suits to fit individual pilots. They must be measured individually. This is likely to take a further 3 months so that we could not reasonably expect sufficient pressure suits to be available to the high altitude squadron before January. At this time we should be getting 10 Spitfire VII's per month so that as I see it any special effort put upon final development and manufacture of pressure suits would not be justified.[23]

There was, however, one further option – to hastily modify an existing fighter for high-altitude interception as an interim solution, pending delivery of the Spitfire Mk VII and Welkin. Fortunately, de Havilland had been working on an experimental high-altitude version of their hugely successful Mosquito multi-role warplane, and priority was now given to making this aircraft ready for operations as quickly as possible.

In early September, a group of senior engineers at de Havilland's factory at Hatfield were called in for a meeting at the main workshop. In the workshop was Mosquito MP469, a PR.Mk VIII version fitted with an experimental pressure cabin. Fred Plumb, the manager of de Havilland's Experimental Flight, addressed the engineers, informing them that they 'were going to start right away working night and day' to modify MP469 so that it could reach the Ju 86R's altitude and shoot it down.[24]

Working flat out, the engineers swapped the nose for one from an NF.Mk II fighter, housing four .303 Browning machine guns, put four-bladed propellers on the two supercharged Merlin 61 engines, with a Marshall compressor fitted to the port engine, and extending the wingtips so that the wingspan was increased from 54 to 59ft. By removing the armour plating, fuselage fuel tanks and outer wing-tanks, they were also able to reduce the weight by around 1,000lbs. After a week of intensive work, this first high-altitude Mosquito, designated the Mk XV, was ready to fly. Geoffrey de Havilland Jnr, son of the aircraft manufacturer's founder, made the first flight in the Mk XV on 14 September, and a day later he reached a height of 43,000ft. On 16 September Pilot Officer Sparrow of No 151 Squadron, on attachment to the Special Service Flight, arrived to take delivery of MP469 to join the effort against the Ju 86Rs from RAF Northolt.

It was an impressive achievement, though by the time MP469 was ready for operations the need for the aircraft had been overtaken by events.

The Special Service Flight

While the workers at de Havilland were busy modifying Mosquito MP469, another initiative to deal with the Ju 86R was being put into action – and this one would finally bring success.

At the beginning of September 1942 an elite new unit, the Special Service Flight, was formed at RAF Northolt, its sole purpose to shoot down the Ju 86Rs. The unit comprised six pilots, chosen according to their physical suitability for extreme altitude flying and commanded by an American, Squadron Leader James 'Jimmy' Nelson. Born in Colorado, Nelson had enlisted in the RAF in early 1941, when the US was still neutral, and served in No 133 (Eagle) Squadron, made up of American volunteers. After the US entered the war and most of the Eagle pilots were absorbed into the USAAF, he remained in the RAF and in January 1944 was awarded the AFC.

Among the pilots selected to join the Special Service Flight was Pilot Officer Prince Emanuel Vladimirovich Galitzine, a Russian-born aristocrat and descendant of Catherine the Great, whose family had fled to England after the 1917 October Revolution. After joining the RAF Volunteer Reserve, he served with No 504 and later the Spitfire Mk IX-equipped No 611 Squadron, based at RAF Redhill in Surrey. On 29 August, shortly before his transfer to the Special Service Flight, Galitzine had a close shave when his Spitfire suffered engine failure during a patrol, leading to a crash-landing, as the 611 Sqn ORB revealed: 'P/O Galitzine, our "Fighting Russian", went over on his "royal back" when trying to force land at Martlesham.' Fortunately, he escaped serious injury.[25]

The group of six pilots were sent to RAE Farnborough for specialised training in flying at altitudes of 40,000ft plus. This included lectures from doctors on the physiological challenges associated with flying in the stratosphere. To condition their bodies for high altitude flight, they had sessions in a decompression chamber and would fly at height without oxygen, pushing themselves further each time. During these flights the doctors impressed upon them the importance of making only 'slow, deliberate' movements in the cockpit to conserve their oxygen. The airmen were also put on a special diet made up of foods in short supply in rationed wartime Britain, including chocolate, eggs, bacon and fresh orange juice, which it was thought would enhance the pilots' stamina at high altitude. Although Galitzine doubted if this diet helped improve their ability to function at extreme altitude, he felt that it did wonders for the pilots' morale.[26]

The aircraft allocated to the Special Service Flight were two heavily modified Spitfire Mk IXs. All equipment considered not absolutely essential was stripped out, including the armour plating and the four .303 Brownings – reducing the armament to just the two Hispano 20mm cannon. The metal propeller was replaced with a much lighter wooden one and the Spitfires were painted in a special lightweight paint, described by Galitzine as 'Cambridge blue'. These modifications reduced the weight by some 450lbs.

Plt Off Galitzine made his first flight in one of the specially lightened Mk IXs on 10 September. Describing its handling as 'absolutely delightful', of the eleven marks of Spitfire he flew during the war he considered the Mk IX 'far and away the best'. Although lacking a pressure cabin, on his second practice flight of the day, to test the cannon while at high altitude, he managed to reach 43,000ft, the electrically-heated flying suit he was provided with keeping him warm.

As the Spitfires consumed much of their fuel in the climb to the Ju 86R's operating altitude, leaving limited time to search for the bandit and make their attack before being forced to return to base, a more precise method of ground control interception was also devised for the Special Service Flight. Codenamed 'Windgap', this entailed having a dedicated controller in a special Area Control Room guide the intercepting Spitfire to its target, using plots of the Ju 86R provided by radar stations along the south coast.[27]

The 'Windgap' system was first tried out on 11 September, when radar picked up a high-flyer heading towards the Yeovil area at a height of 43,000ft. One of the Special Service Flight's Mk IXs was scrambled and managed to reach 45,000ft. Frustratingly, however, the radio failed and so the ground controller was unable to direct the pilot to the bandit's position. The Ju 86R, flown by Altrogge, dropped its bomb on Parkstone in Poole, killing five people. A pair of No 501's stripped-down Spitfire Vbs were also sent up. 'They gained on E/A at first but were later out-climbed. The ack-ack opened up from Poole and bursts were uncomfortably near one Spitfire,' stated the Squadron ORB.[28]

The next day Sommer and Goetz took off from Beauvais at 0825 hrs on another mission, flying in T5+PM, their target this time being Cardiff. Half an hour later they were picked up by British radar near Rouen at a height of 26,000ft and climbing. Once at a height of 42,000ft they crossed the English Channel. Two pilots of No 421 (RCAF) Squadron, who had been detached to RAF Colerne two days earlier, were the first to be scrambled in response to the incoming raider in their Spitfire Vbs, spotting the Ju 86R near the Isle of Wight. Neither fighter could reach the bomber and eventually they were forced to break off the pursuit and head back to base.

At around 0950 hrs T5+PM reached Southampton and headed northwest towards Cardiff. Twenty-five minutes earlier, Pilot Officer Galitzine, who was on standby that morning in Spitfire BF273, was scrambled from Northolt as the Ju 86R headed across the Channel. Climbing quickly to 15,000ft, he was ordered by ground control onto a south-westerly heading and, after being given several course corrections, eventually caught sight of black smoke trails above him while flying at 41,000ft north of Southampton. 'I turned to starboard to maintain climbing speed and avoid overshooting and came level at 42,000ft with the a/c – which I recognised as a Ju 86P,' Galitzine confirmed in his combat report.[29]

Sommer, who was serving as observer, was scanning the sky behind them when he spotted a condensation trail. Initially, he was unconcerned, assuming that the trail was caused by the second Ju 86R, which had been due to take off just after them. But as the aircraft came into view, much to his dismay he realised it was a Spitfire. And it was closing in fast. He alerted his pilot Goetz, who was unperturbed by the news. RAF fighters had, after all, attempted to reach their altitude to intercept them every time they flew over England – without success. But then Sommer told him this Spitfire was continuing to climb and had almost reached their altitude. Thinking his observer's eyes 'must have been playing tricks on him,' Goetz leaned over to look through Sommer's window. 'To my horror,' he recalled, 'I saw a Spitfire, a little above us and still climbing.'[30]

To lighten their weight and gain more altitude, Sommer released the 551lb bomb – which landed near Salisbury. Goetz, meanwhile, opened up the air vent to reduce air pressure in the cabin, to prevent sudden decompression should they be hit by enemy fire, and both crewmen put on their oxygen masks. They turned back for France, gaining more height in the hope of outclimbing the Spitfire.

Galitzine jettisoned his 30-gallon slipper fuel tank and continued climbing, matching and then surpassing the Ju 86R's height by 200ft before making his first attack, as he described in his combat report:

> I got slightly to starboard and 2/300ft above and came in to within 600 yds. I dived down on him out of the sun and from 200 yds, dead astern, I opened fire with a 3 sec burst, closing to 150 yds. My port gun then jammed and I flew into his slipstream, my windscreen becoming completely obscured.

Sommer warned Goetz of the attack, who made a tight evasive turn, but not fast enough to avoid one of Galitzine's 20mm cannon shells, which tore through the Ju 86R's port wing and exited through the leading edge. Galitzine, his view out of the cockpit obscured by the bomber's slipstream, temporarily lost sight of his target. When it had cleared, he 'picked up the E/A again and, getting into position for attack, dived fairly steeply on him from astern with an A.S.I of 135'. He opened fire again with his one functioning cannon, but his Spitfire went into a spin and lost height. Undeterred, Galitzine climbed back up to 44,000ft and made another attack. 'Climbing again, I waited until he was in sight and dived on him, closing to 100 yds and opened fire with my starboard cannon only. This pulled my a/c round and caused me to drop into his slipstream again with the usual result – my windscreen became clouded,' he reported.[31]

Galitzine caught up with the fleeing bomber and made a fourth and final attack, firing his single operable cannon, which once again caused his Spitfire to yaw and lose altitude. Goetz, meanwhile, made for a layer of cloud below in the hope of shaking off his determined pursuer. During the dive the Junkers' engines flamed out, trailing grey smoke. Goetz successfully restarted the engines in the warmer air at lower altitude and headed back across the Channel at low level.

After a running battle lasting some forty-five minutes, Galitzine, running perilously low on fuel, was finally forced to abandon the chase when he was around twenty-five miles from the French coast and turn back for home. Lacking the fuel to make it back to Northolt, he landed instead at Tangmere, sixty miles farther south, at 1100 hrs.

It had been a truly heroic effort, but Galitzine was frustrated that the Ju 86R had slipped away, believing that had it not been for the cannon stoppage he suffered during the battle, he would have downed the bomber.[32]

Unknown to Galitzine, however, his initial attack had been more successful than he realised at the time. Goetz made an emergency landing at Caen-Carpiquet airfield and he and Sommer carried out a cursory inspection of the damaged wing. Judging the aircraft safe to fly, they flew on to Beauvais, over 100 miles away. There, a more thorough examination of the damage inflicted by Galitzine's single 20mm cannon shell revealed just how fortunate Sommer and Goetz had been. Inside the port wing they discovered that the shell had punched a large hole through the vertical member of the main spar. 'Luckily,' commented Sommer, 'it had held during our dive and tight turns, both of which had exceeded the specified safety limits.'

The next day Leutnant Sommer was summoned to the headquarters of KG 6 for a meeting with the commanding officer, Oberst Walter Storp, who was enthusiastic about the operations of the *Höhenkampf Kommando*. Unaware of the close call Sommer and Goetz had experienced on their last mission, Storp informed him that due to the unit's success there were plans to increase its size to a full squadron and rename it the 14th *Staffel*. However, 'when I told him of what had happened the day before and that the British now had fighters that could reach our operational height, he immediately saw the end of his dream,' revealed Sommer.[33]

Its period of immunity from interception at an end, the *Höhenkampf Kommando* was disbanded. The four Ju 86Rs were put into storage at the old Zeppelin hangars at Orly and the crews reassigned to other squadrons – Altrogge resumed his work as a test pilot at Rechlin, where he was killed while flying a prototype of the unorthodox Dornier Do 335 fighter in April 1944, while Sommer and Goetz would continue flying together until September 1944, including carrying out the first operational jet reconnaissance missions, over Normandy in the Arado Ar 234.

Before it was disbanded, however, there was to be one final sortie by the Ju 86R over England, its purpose to establish the maximum altitude that could be attained by the RAF's high-flying Spitfires. Sommer and Werner Altrogge undertook the risky mission on 2 October 1942, taking off from Beauvais without a bomb and a reduced fuel load, which would allow them to add an extra 2,500ft to their ceiling. Over England they reached the incredible height of 48,000ft and penetrated as far as Tunbridge Wells before turning back. Six Spitfires were scrambled in response but the nearest any of them got was 3,000ft below Sommer and Altrogge's aircraft, this Spitfire going into a spin after firing a burst from his cannon. One of the other pursuing Spitfires was accidentally shot down by 'friendly' flak.

A high-altitude night interceptor

Unaware that the Germans had decided to indefinitely suspend the Ju 86R raids, in Britain fears persisted that the Luftwaffe would soon resume the high-altitude bombing offensive, possibly switching to night raids and employing radar-jamming equipment to give them added protection. These fears prompted discussion among the RAF's top brass over how to meet this potential threat. What was required, wrote AVM Sorley on 19 September, was an aircraft:

> having a speed at 30,000ft in excess of 350 mph, and a ceiling not less than 44,000ft, and preferably 46,000ft, armed with 2 x 20mm guns or 4 x .303. The aircraft will be required with pressure cabin and carry V.H.F. RT and 10 cm A.I., with devices for homing on to an airborne jammer. Violent fighting manoeuvres will not be required for this aircraft and, consequently, factors can be reduced to minimum acceptable limits.

These requirements, he suggested, could be met by the 'specially developed Mosquito which has done so remarkably well already'.[34]

Bottomley agreed, writing on 5 October that, 'The development of the Mosquito as a high-altitude fighter would provide us with the only aircraft with a ceiling of 44,000ft capable of taking the pilot operated Centimetre A.I. in the immediate future', and that it would constitute 'our only safeguard by night'.[35]

Work immediately commenced on adapting Mosquito MP469 into a night-fighter. A new nose containing the AI Mk VIII centimetric radar was fitted, with the armament relocated in a gunpack beneath the fuselage. Now redesignated the NF.Mk XV, MP469 was sent to Boscombe Down for evaluation. The test pilot reported that, 'The handling is satisfactory, there being no tendency for any of the controls to freeze up at height, nor is the extent of icing inside the cabin at all serious', and noted that 'there is no marked difference in behaviour when compared with normal Mosquito aircraft'. It was also established that the Mk XV could climb to 30,000ft in just ten minutes.[36]

In February 1943, MP469 was issued to No 85 Squadron at RAF Hunsdon, under the command of the legendary night fighter ace Wing Commander John 'Cats Eyes' Cunningham, where in one flight in June 1943 it reached 45,000ft during a misting test. Soon after it was sent to RAF Turnhouse near Edinburgh to provide defence of Scotland and northern England from any high-flying enemy intruders, which proved notable by their absence.

Four more Mosquitoes, all B.Mk IV bomber variants, were converted to Mk XV standard, finished in a dark blue colour scheme and with an even greater wingspan of 62.5ft. Richard Whittingham, a Flight Inspector at de Havilland's, was taken on a flight in one of these Mosquitoes, DZ417, on 16 February 1943, with company test pilot George Errington at the controls.

Errington took the Mosquito up to 42,000ft, Whittingham writing that it was 'a marvellous experience and one which I shall never forget. My abiding memory is how black the sky was looking upwards at that altitude.'[37]

Fortunately, the high-altitude night bombing threat never materialised. In the course of the Luftwaffe's brief high-altitude daylight bombing campaign of August–September 1942, a total of 7,700lbs of bombs – less than the average bombload of a single Lancaster bomber – was dropped in the 14 raids carried out by the Ju 86Rs. With the exception of the Bristol raid on 28 August, the *Höhenkampf Kommando* had inflicted few casualties and little damage. But this small unit had succeeded in causing fear and alarm to the enemy, as well as tying down considerable British air defence resources, without suffering any loss to themselves.

Chapter Nine

Luftwaffe *Höhenjägers*

T he Luftwaffe's successful use of the Ju 86R to bomb
England in 1942 led to fears among senior Nazis that
the Allies would reciprocate by expanding their own
escalating bombing campaign to include high–altitude raids
carried out by fleets of pressurised heavy bombers, which
their current standard fighters for the air defence of Germany
by day, the Bf 109 and Fw 190, would be incapable of shooting
down. These concerns were raised by Field Marshal Erhard
Milch, Inspector-General of the Luftwaffe, when he addressed
a conference held in August 1943 to discuss German aircraft
production. 'We are very much afraid,' he told his audience,
'that enemy bombers will be appearing at very great altitudes
above the effective ceiling of the 109 and 190. These types
could reach such heights, but only for a very short time, just
because their endurance is so limited.'[1] Almost a year earlier,
Goering had expressed similar fears at a gathering of senior
figures from the German aviation industry at Karinhall,
his country retreat in Brandenburg, telling them he wanted
'high–altitude fighters that operate at 14, 15 km height, where
we expect the bombers of the future, to shoot down those
bombers'.[2]

Sky-high Wimpeys and Lancs

Their fears were well-founded, for the Allies were indeed developing a range of stratospheric bombers.

The British Air Ministry's interest in high-altitude bombers dated back to the outset of the war. Bomber Command had learned the hard way through bruising experiences in the first months of the war that sending out unescorted bombers on daylight raids against well-defended enemy targets was to invite disaster. One such raid, on 18 December 1939, resulted in twelve out of a force of twenty-four Wellingtons sent out to attack German shipping at Wilhelmshaven being shot down by Bf 109s and 110s. While Bomber Command's switch to night-bombing had initially cut losses, as the Luftwaffe began introducing increasingly effective radar-equipped night-fighters, able to seek out and destroy British bombers on the darkest of nights, losses again mounted. Pressurised bombers with a very high service ceiling were seen as a potential remedy to the situation. Having settled on a policy of area bombing in early 1942, the fact that obtaining any degree of accuracy when bombing from 40,000ft and above was virtually impossible was regarded as largely irrelevant.

As the most numerous and effective of the RAF's bombers in the early years of the war, the Vickers Wellington was the obvious choice to be adapted for the high-altitude role. Designed by Sir Barnes Wallis, of 'bouncing bomb' fame, the Wellington – affectionately known as the 'Wimpey' to its crews – entered service in October 1938. Its geodetic structure made it capable of absorbing substantial battle damage and it could carry 4,500lbs of bombs. Over 11,000 were produced, more than any other British bomber, and it served from the first day of the war to the last.

Vickers' proposal to meet Air Ministry Specification B.23/39 of 1939, requiring a high-altitude bomber with pressure cabin, which should have a cruising altitude of 35,000ft, was the Wellington Mk V. Differences from previous marks included an increased wingspan and the replacement of the standard Wellington's Pegasus engines with Hercules Mk VIIIs. The incorporation of a pressure cabin to accommodate a four-man crew necessitated a complete redesign of the nose section, giving the Mk V a somewhat whale-like appearance. Another distinctive feature was the fighter-type canopy atop the fuselage. The prototype, R3298, first flew on 25 September 1940, from RAF Squire's Gate in Blackpool. But it was quickly superseded by the Mk VI, an improved version which swapped the Hercules engines for the Merlin 60.

An initial order for sixty-four was placed, which were built at the Vickers factory in Weybridge, Surrey. But testing of the Mk VI with the High Altitude Flight at Boscombe Down did not go smoothly. The pilot's position, set far back from the nose, made take-offs and landings tricky, while engine lubricants tended to freeze at high altitude. Then, on 12 July 1942, a test flight in Wellington W5795 ended in tragedy. After reaching 35,500ft, the Wellington went into a steep dive and crashed into a field near Ilkeston, Derbyshire. Decades later an eyewitness, Connie Shooter, recalled watching the stricken aircraft 'rolling over and over like a barrel,' before breaking up and crashing to the ground.[3] The pilot, Squadron Leader Cyril

Colmore, and his crew – Flying Officer Kenneth Radford, Flight Sergeants Ronald Gillot and Arthur Smith, and the HAF's Deputy Technical Officer Clifford Abbott – were all killed. An investigation concluded that the most likely cause of the crash was one of the starboard engine's propellers breaking away, smashing into the cabin and injuring Colmore.

A plan to use the Mk VIs as pathfinders, marking targets with flares for the follow-on bomber force, was dropped. By the time it was ready for operations, this role was already being fulfilled very effectively by the Mosquito. Instead, four of the production aircraft were assigned to No 109 Squadron in 1942 to train crews on the Gee navigation aid and for trials of Oboe, the codename of a new radar-based navigation system designed to increase bombing accuracy at night and in poor visibility, which was developed by the Telecommunications Research Establishment at Malvern. In 1942 the TRE scientists required a high-altitude aircraft as a testbed for Oboe. But 'we couldn't find an aircraft to fly high enough,' explained Francis Jones, one of the scientists involved in developing Oboe. 'What the Air Force offered us was a thing called a Wellington VI, a pressurised aircraft. Terrible thing to see out of. I myself flew in it about three times. One of them exploded over Boscombe Down. After that it was grounded.'[4] The Wellingtons were replaced in the high-altitude Oboe test flights by the new Mosquito Mk IV.

A proposal was also put forward to convert Britain's most successful heavy bomber of the war, the legendary Avro Lancaster, for high-altitude work. Unlike the Wellington Mk VI, however, the Avro Model 684 failed to reach the production stage. Roy Chadwick, chief designer at Avro, began work on a pressurised variant of the Lancaster in 1941, even before the standard bomber had entered service. The Model 684 would do away with all defensive armament, while a fifth engine, a Rolls Royce Merlin 45, would be mounted in the fuselage above the main spar, driving a supercharger. But with Avro fully committed to production of the standard versions of the Lancaster, the Model 684 was seen as an unnecessary distraction and the project was cancelled.

The 'Victory Bomber'

The most ambitious British 'Strato' bomber project of the Second World War was the brainchild of Barnes Wallis. In the early months of the war the famed aeronautical engineer and inventor was working on a concept for massively destructive 'earthquake' bombs, which would eventually emerge as the 12,000lb Tallboy and its even more formidable big brother, the 22,000lb Grand Slam. A handful of bombers, each carrying one of these bombs, could, Wallis believed, destroy an area of sixteen square kilometres.

As no bomber then in service could carry a bomb of such weight, he set about designing what he dubbed a 'monster bomber' – a six-engine behemoth, weighing 50 tons fully laden (the Wellington, by contrast, weighed in at 12 tons), with a wingspan of 172ft, a ceiling of 45,000ft and a range of 4,000 miles. Christened the Victory Bomber, it would feature cabin pressurisation, Wallis' trademark geodetic structure and, as its altitude was expected to protect it from fighter interception, light armament consisting of only a four-gun tail turret. Ranging over enemy territory 'at their leisure and in daylight', Wallis argued the crew could safely hit their target from 40,000ft. To resolve the problem of bombing accuracy at very high altitude, Wallis believed that a gyroscopic bombsight would allow the crew to drop their bomb within 150 yards of the target. He assured his bosses at Vickers that the bomber had the potential to be 'the instrument which will enable us to bring the war to a quick conclusion'.[5]

The concept gained the support of Vickers' managing director Sir Charles Craven and plans for the Victory Bomber were submitted to Lord Beaverbrook in July 1940, who was attracted to the proposal. A wooden mock-up was produced for wind tunnel testing, but the ambitious project would advance no further than that. The Air Ministry decided that the resources required to produce such a machine would place too great a strain on Britain's already overstretched aviation industry and in May 1941 Wallis was informed by government scientific adviser and chairman of the Aeronautical Research Committee Sir Henry Tizard that the Victory Bomber project had been rejected. When the Tallboy and Grand Slam bombs did eventually enter service, they would be carried in specially adapted Lancasters, taking out key targets in the last months of the war, including V1 launch sites, U-boat pens and Hitler's mighty battleship, the *Tirpitz*.

Vickers would, however, have one final attempt at producing a high-altitude heavy bomber during the war. This project had its origins in a 1941 specification (B.5/41, later revised to B.3/42) for a high-altitude heavy bomber equipped with a pressure cabin, with a cruising altitude of 31,000ft and a ceiling of 38,500ft. Vickers, which was already working on the pressurised version of the trusty Wellington, responded with a proposal designed by Barnes Wallis and Rex Pierson for a four-engine development of the Warwick. The Warwick was essentially a slightly enlarged Wellington, which from 1942 saw service with RAF Transport and Coastal Command. The new aircraft would feature very large elliptical wings, four Merlin 61 engines and, like the Wellington Mk V and VI, a fighter-type cockpit mounted atop the nose. It also shared the same geodetic structure employed on the Wellington. The defensive armament would comprise two .303 machine guns in the nose and a pair of 20mm cannon contained in barbettes mounted at the rear of the outboard engine nacelles, controlled remotely by a gunner sitting in the pressurised tail section.

Impressed by the design, the Air Ministry ordered two prototypes (later increased to three), and it was given the designation Vickers Type 433 Windsor. These were constructed at the Vickers facility at Foxwarren – where Vickers' Type 432 fighter had been built – and the first prototype (DW506) made its maiden flight on 23 October 1943 from RAE Farnborough, with Vickers' chief test pilot, the famous Joseph 'Mutt' Summers, at the controls. The second prototype (DW512) introduced some changes, the most significant of these being the replacement of the Merlin 61 powerplants with the Merlin 85, and undertook its first flight on 15 February 1944, while the third and final example (NK136) carried out its debut flight on 11 July 1944. The armament was installed on this third prototype in January 1945.

Eric Brown was among the test pilots who flew the Windsor from Farnborough. His opinion of the aircraft was generally favourable, though he did note one alarming flight characteristic during the trials:

> The wings flapped in flight. At full load on take-off the wingtips flexed as much as six feet. She went along looking like a huge, gentle seagull. The flexing of the geodetically-constructed wings had an adverse effect on performance, but I enjoyed flying this aircraft.[6]

More than 130 test flights were carried out. On one of these, on 2 March 1944, DW506 was written off after making a forced landing at RAF Grove in Berkshire due to engine problems.

During the testing phase, Air Ministry interest in the Vickers Windsor steadily declined. An initial order for 300 placed in April 1943 was cut to 100 in November 1944, and later reduced even further. The fact of the matter was that the Windsor was surplus to requirements – the Lancaster was meeting all Bomber Command's needs in the heavy bomber role admirably, and in any case there was little prospect of the Windsor reaching operational status before the defeat of Nazi Germany. 'It really arrived too late on the war scene to be adopted for service,' said Brown.[7]

Development continued without any great urgency, with the possibility of deploying the type to the Far East against Japan. The abrupt end of the Pacific War in August 1945 put paid to these plans and the Windsor was officially cancelled in

November. The two surviving prototypes, along with two more which were under construction, were eventually broken up.

Dragons and Super Marauders

Having put into commercial service the world's first pressurised airliner, the United States was inevitably at the forefront of developing high-altitude bombers equipped with pressure cabins, even before the country had entered the war. In August 1939 the USAAC issued Specification XC-214 for a high-altitude, twin-engine medium bomber. North American Aviation and the Glenn L. Martin Company responded with, respectively, the Model NA-63, allocated the designation XB-28 'Dragon', and the Model 182, designated the XB-27. North American's proposal was selected on 15 November 1939 and the following February a contract for two prototypes was awarded.

Originally conceived simply as a pressurised version of the same company's B-25 Mitchell bomber, the finished aircraft was an almost completely new design. The XB-28 was powered by a pair of Pratt & Whitney R-2800 turbo-supercharged engines and flew for the first time on 26 April 1942, from Mines Field in Los Angeles. The second prototype, a reconnaissance variant, began flight testing a year later. Despite this aircraft crashing off the southern Californian coast in August 1943 (both crewmen successfully baling out), the XB-28 was judged to be a successful design, with few vices.

But shifting attitudes within the USAAF – as the USAAC had by now been renamed – over the validity of extremely high-altitude bombing in the European theatre, with the lack of accuracy obtainable at great height conflicting with the Air Force's doctrine of precision bombing against purely military and industrial targets, led to a re-evaluation of the need for a pressurised medium bomber. And so, in late 1943, the XB-28 was cancelled.

The USAAF did, however, retain an interest in pressurised heavy bombers, for use against Japan. Having lost out to North American Aviation in the high-altitude medium bomber project, the Martin Company gained the interest of the Air Force with its proposal for a heavy bomber version of its B-26 Marauder. Intended to be powered by four Wright R-2600 engines and carry a bombload of 12,000lbs up to a maximum altitude of 39,000ft, the XB-33A 'Super Marauder' sufficiently impressed the Air Force for a contract for 400 to be placed in January 1942. But with the Martin factory in Omaha, Nebraska at full capacity after the company was sub-contracted to help build Boeing B-29s, which had been accorded the highest priority, the contract was cancelled in November before any Super Marauders had been built.

A Nazi Welkin

By early 1942 reports were filtering back to Germany that the British and Americans were working on a variety of high-altitude bomber projects. Much of the information the Germans gleaned on the US projects came from open sources – American aviation magazines which freely published details of US military aircraft under development. In response, a meeting was held on 12 May 1942 chaired by Milch and attended by senior figures from the RLM and Luftwaffe – including the legendary ace and Inspector of Fighters Adolf Galland, as well as the Luftwaffe's Chief of the General Staff Hans Jeschonnek – to discuss the threat and the possible requirement of specialised high-altitude fighters (*höhenjägers*) to defend the Reich from such machines.

After discussing the practical problems associated with intercepting aircraft at very high altitudes with the fighters then available to the Luftwaffe, the meeting turned to a discussion of the means of improving the high-altitude performance and reducing the climb time of the Bf 109G, the latest version of the Luftwaffe's standard fighter. The addition of the GM-1 nitrous oxide boost system, observed RLM engineer Walter Friebel, 'has great advantages for short-term increase in speed at high altitude, but due to the large additional weight only small benefits to improve climbing performance'. Friebel was optimistic that the new Daimler-Benz engine optimised for high altitude which was then under development, the DB 628, installed in the 109G airframe with reduced armament 'should have the greatest prospects for the preparation of a good high-altitude fighter', and urged that work on this engine should be accelerated.[8]

Besides a 109 optimised for higher altitudes, Friebel also suggested consideration should be given to developing 'a special high-altitude fighter, which can be designed properly for maximum altitude' – an all-new aircraft designed from the outset as an extreme altitude bomber interceptor.[9] Others, like Walter Storp, an experienced bomber pilot who was serving in a staff appointment in the RLM at the time, argued that the focus for the time-being should be on adapting the 109, so that it could 'get safely to 13,000 to 14,000m'.[10] Eight days later the already overburdened Messerschmitt company received an order to produce a '*spezial höhenjäger*'. The programme would eventually split into two separate lines of development: a high-altitude version of the Bf 109 and an entirely new aircraft, the Me 155.

For the *höhenjäger* variant of the 109, the 'H' model, Messerschmitt modified the airframe by extending the wingspan from just over 32 to 39ft and moving the undercarriage oleos further outboard. To meet the RLM's specified maximum altitude requirement of 15,000 metres [49,200ft], the new DB 628 engine was chosen as the powerplant. But this larger and heavier engine necessitated significant alterations to the 109 airframe, including an enlarged tailplane.

Constantly changing RLM requirements and Messerschmitt's heavy workload meant that progress on the 109 *höhenjäger* project was slow. A small number of pre-production Bf 109Hs were produced for flight testing in 1943 and the type first flew in November, with Messerschmitt test pilot Fritz Wendel at the controls. During tests the 109H managed to reach an absolute ceiling of 50,800ft but, as the British were experiencing with their Westland Welkin, the pilots encountered serious stability problems at such altitudes, particularly wing flutter. On one test flight in April 1944 the port wing was ripped off during a dive. The testing programme was further disrupted when a major Allied air raid on Messerschmitt's Augsburg factory on 25 February 1944 destroyed one of the prototypes. Persistent issues with stability led to the abandonment of work on the

109H as an interceptor a few months later. However, as we have previously seen, several of those already produced were modified for use in the high-altitude reconnaissance role.

Messerschmitt's other *höhenjäger* project, the Me 155, had a particularly convoluted history, even by the standards of Nazi Germany's wartime aviation projects. The designation had originally been applied to a carrier fighter Messerschmitt was commissioned to produce in May 1942 to serve aboard Germany's aircraft carrier, the *Graf Zeppelin*. But by January 1943 work on the *Graf Zeppelin* had ground to a halt due to Hitler's loss of faith in the Kriegsmarine's surface fleet and the Me 155 designation was assigned to the *'extremen höhenjäger'* (extreme high-altitude fighter) the Luftwaffe was demanding.

Messerschmitt, however, was more interested in developing a high-altitude version of its troubled Bf 209, the intended successor to the 109, than in designing an all-new interceptor. But RLM enthusiasm for a 209 *höhenjäger* was lukewarm, not least because the entire 209 programme had become mired in development difficulties (which would eventually lead to its cancellation by Goering in December 1943), and the idea was dropped.

With Messerschmitt severely overstretched by all its commitments and having little time to devote to the Me 155, in mid-1943 Blohm & Voss was brought in to alleviate the burden. Besides its main work as a shipbuilder, the company was best known for its seaplanes. After repeatedly clashing with the Messerschmitt team over the design, Blohm & Voss, which had ample spare capacity following the cancellation of its BV

138, 222 and 238 seaplanes in 1943, eventually took over sole responsibility for the entire Me 155 project.

The company's chief designer Dr Richard Vogt and his team set about a complete redesign of the 155, which was eventually rechristened the BV 155 in early 1944. What Dr Vogt produced was a large single-seat fighter with a wingspan of just over 67ft, distinguished by two large radiators positioned midway along each wing. Armament was to consist of three Mk 108 30mm cannon. For the powerplant, Blohm & Voss settled on the DB 603U engine, with the Heinkel-Hirth TKL 15 turbo-supercharger, which they believed would allow the 155 to reach the RLM's ambitious specified maximum altitude.

Besides the Blohm & Voss project, the Focke-Wulf company was also working on a design to meet the Luftwaffe's high-altitude interceptor requirement. The solution proposed by Focke-Wulf's chief designer Kurt Tank was to heavily modify his highly successful Fw 190 fighter.

Tank had been well aware of the 190's limitations at high-altitude, the performance of its BMW 801 radial engine dropping off significantly above 25,000ft, and foresaw the need for a version able to operate effectively at higher altitudes.

In a 1975 interview Tank recalled:

Early in 1941, before the Fw 190 entered service, I had spoken to Luftwaffe Generals [Ernst] Udet and Jeschonnek about it. I said they should put the Jumo 213 high-altitude engine, then being bench-tested at Junkers, into series production so that we could have a

high-altitude version of the Fw 190 ready in case it was
needed. General Hans Jeschonnek, then Chief of Staff
of the Luftwaffe, had replied: 'What is the point of that?
We are not fighting any air battles at high altitude!'[11]

Consequently, according to Tank, development of high-altitude
engines in Germany was set back by a year.

To speed up the new type's entry into service, as many
Fw 190 parts as possible were to be utilised. The resulting
Ta 152 essentially resembled a stretched 190, with lengthened
fuselage and nose (to accommodate the Jumo 213E powerplant).
The wingspan was also increased, from the 190's 34 to 47ft.
Armament comprised three cannon – a Mk 108 30mm mounted
in the engine block, firing through the propeller hub, and an
MG 151 20mm cannon in each wing. Several standard fighter
versions, the Ta 152A, B and C models, were also planned, but
in the end only the 152H *höhenjäger* variant, with pressurised
cockpit, made it into production.

By early 1944, however, with the feared Allied high-altitude
bombing offensive having failed to materialise, Luftwaffe
interest in specialised extreme altitude interceptors was waning.
The BV 155 project in particular, which was progressing at a
very slow pace, was in danger of being cancelled altogether.
The future of the aircraft was raised at a meeting attended by
senior figures of the RLM and the Luftwaffe held in March,
which was chaired by Milch. Although avoiding outright
cancellation, the meeting concluded that the type was no
longer a priority, Milch stating that 'prototyping of the Me
155 can be stopped'.[12]

B-29s over the Fatherland?

But no sooner had this decision been reached than the need for a *höhenjäger* had to be reassessed after disturbing news reached Germany of possible American plans to unleash a fearsome new weapon. In February 1944, bombers of the US Eighth Air Force dropped copies of the *Sternenbanner* ('Star-Spangled Banner') propaganda leaflet over German cities, warning the German people that they would soon face a new aircraft, 'the biggest bomber in the world', which could carry 'four times the bombload of the current Flying Fortress'.[13] Although the leaflet didn't name this new bomber, the Nazis realised it must be referring to the Boeing B-29 Superfortress, the first bomber in the world to enter operational service that was designed from the outset to incorporate fully pressurised crew cabin compartments.

To give substance to this threat, on 6 March 1944 an early production model of the B-29, named 'Hobo Queen', landed at RAF St Mawgan in Cornwall. For the next four weeks the 'Hobo Queen' made a high-profile tour of RAF and USAAF bomber bases in England, where the aircraft was inspected by the likes of Churchill, Eisenhower, commander of the Eighth Air Force General Carl Spaatz, and Air Marshal Sir Arthur Tedder. The object of the exercise was to convince the Nazis that the B-29 was to be used against Germany.

Of course, the USAAF had no real intention of deploying the B-29 to the European theatre. But this disinformation exercise helped revive Nazi fears of enemy high-altitude bombing. As a consequence, new momentum was injected into the *höhenjäger* programme. Work on the BV 155 was accelerated and in July the original order for five prototypes was increased to seven. The RLM also invited Heinkel to join the race to meet the *extremen höhenjäger* requirement. Heinkel's P.1076 was designed by Siegfried Günter, who had also worked on the He 111 bomber, and was based largely on his pre-war He 100 fighter (which had failed to secure a production order). The P.1076 would have featured contra-rotating propellers and a wing swept forward at eight degrees, with the DB 603N providing the power. Work on the P.1076, however, began too late in the war for it to progress beyond a set of incomplete drawings.

The first BV 155 prototype, the 155 V1 (Werk Nr 360051) was completed in February 1945 and on the 8th Blohm & Voss' chief test pilot Helmut Rodig made the first flight. He identified various problems, including inadequate brakes, a faulty airspeed indicator and a coolant leak from the starboard radiator, which forced him to cut short the flight. 'An assessment of the flight characteristics, even only a rough one,' Rodig reported, 'cannot be given under these circumstances.'[14] Two days later Rodig conducted a second test flight. Among the problems noted this time were a lack of longitudinal stability and excessively high oil temperature, which again curtailed the flight. A third, and what would prove to be final, test flight was carried out by Rodig on 28 February. While some of the issues he had highlighted in the previous two flights had been resolved, he found that others persisted, including overly heavy rudder controls and faults with the landing gear.

In spite of the rapidly deteriorating war situation, a further programme of test flights for March and April was planned, but these would not be carried out, nor would the two other prototypes still under construction be completed. The sole complete BV 155 prototype was damaged in a crash landing on 23 April, minutes after pilot Kurt Reuth had taken off from Neumünster on a ferry flight, the cause apparently being undercarriage failure. In June a US technical team from the CIOS, assisted by RAF Flight Lieutenant Littlefield, carried out an initial inspection of the second prototype, which was nearing completion when the Blohm & Voss factory at Finkenwerder in Hamburg was captured by British forces on 3 May. The aircraft was disassembled and, along with spare parts and technical documents, shipped back to the UK. Reassembled, it was put on display along with other captured enemy aircraft at the German Aircraft Exhibition, which was held at Farnborough between October and November 1945. In January 1946 it was shipped to the US aboard the SS *Port Fairy* and sent to the Foreign Evaluation Center at Freeman Field, Indiana, for further study.[15]

Focke-Wulf's rival *höhenjäger*, the Ta 152H, did at least see some limited operational service – albeit briefly and not in the high-altitude bomber destroyer role for which it had originally been envisaged.

In December 1943 six prototypes of the Ta 152H were ordered. An evaluation unit, *Erprobungskommando* Ta 152, was set up at Rechlin, with the first flights carried out in early November 1944. These flights revealed that the Ta 152H's high-altitude performance was exceptional, achieving a top speed of 469 mph at 44,300ft and reaching a maximum altitude of 49,540ft. With the war situation deteriorating rapidly, that same month the Ta 152H was ordered into production at Focke-Wulf's factory at Cottbus in eastern Germany. In December 1944 Kurt Tank himself was able to demonstrate the superior performance of his latest creation when, just after taking off from Lagenhagen, near Hanover, on a flight to Cottbus in an unarmed Ta 152, he was alerted by ground control that a pair of P-51s were approaching. As the American fighters came in to attack, Tank opened up the throttle and left the P-51s trailing in his wake.[16] It is believed that a total of forty-four production Ta 152H aircraft, along with a further eleven prototypes, were completed before advancing Soviet forces brought production at Cottbus to an end in March 1945.

On 16 January 1945, fourteen Ta 152Hs fresh off the production line were destroyed in a strafing attack by USAAF P-38s and P-51s on the airfield at Neuhausen. Sixteen of the remaining completed Ta 152Hs were operated by Stab/JG 301 – a former *Wilde Sau* unit – which became the only frontline squadron to equip with the type. JG 301 received their first twelve examples at Alteno in eastern Germany in late January and had the job of protecting Luftwaffe fighter airfields in the area from roving Allied fighters.

Advances by the Red Army forced JG 301 to move to Sachau airfield near Berlin on 19 February, and on 1 March Oberfeldwebel Josef 'Jupp' Keil achieved an unconfirmed P-51 'kill'. However, the unfamiliar shape of the new fighter was causing recognition problems among their fellow Luftwaffe pilots. On 2 March, Bf 109s attacked several Ta 152Hs after mistaking them for Allied fighters, though the 152Hs were able to avoid being shot down by exploiting their superior performance.

Over the next few weeks there were further moves for the unit, first to Stendel, west of Berlin, on 13 March and then to Neustadt-Glewe on 10 April. That day another probable 'kill', this time of a P-47, was claimed by Keil. Soon after another of JG 301's pilots, Oberfeldwebel Willi Reschke, got the opportunity to demonstrate the qualities of the Ta 152H when he tangled with one of the Allies' most potent fighters. On the evening of 14 April, a pair of Hawker Tempests of No 486 (RNZAF) Sqn on an armed reconnaissance over the town of Ludwigslust was intercepted by three Ta 152Hs. Reschke zeroed in on one of the Tempests, striking it in the rear fuselage and tail during a twisting dogfight at heights as low as 30ft. Though the German's guns then jammed, he had inflicted enough damage to cause the Tempest to crash into a wood, killing its pilot Warrant Officer Owen Mitchell. The 486 Sqn ORB stated that Mitchell was last seen duelling 'with three Fw 190s [*sic*], almost on the deck'.[17] Mitchell's body was recovered from the crash site by the Germans the next day and buried with military honours. Reschke later wrote that at no time during the battle did he feel that his fighter had reached the limits of its performance.[18]

But the Luftwaffe pilots didn't have it all their own way that day. A second pair of Tempests from 486 Sqn, flown by Wing Commander Richard Brooker DSO DFC and Warrant Officer Bill Shaw, spotted one of the Ta 152Hs flying at low level a few miles east of Ludwigslust and went in to the attack. Shaw described the action, in which he misidentified his prey as an Fw 190, in his combat report:

The 190 broke when we were out of range and as I could see that my No 1 [Wing Commander Brooker] would be unable to attack I dropped my tanks and climbed for height. As the enemy aircraft straightened out east I dived on it passing my No 1. This time the 190 broke rather later and again to port and I was able to pull my bead through until he disappeared beneath my nose. It was a full deflection shot and I opened fire when I judged I had two radii deflection on him. I fired a long burst and then broke upwards to observe the results. As the 190 came in sight again I saw the flash of a strike just forward of the cockpit. An instant later flames appeared from the port side and, enveloped in flames, the 190 went down in a gradual straight dive to the deck. I saw it crash in a field and explode.[19]

It's believed that Shaw's victim was Oberfeldwebel Sepp Sattler, whose Ta 152H crashed in the area at about the same time.

Another of the 486 Sqn pilots, Flying Officer Sidney Short – who was flying alongside Warrant Officer Mitchell – claimed damage to another of the Ta 152Hs, though he mistook his target for a Bf 109. He later reported firing 'a burst with about 45° off. The 109 flew through [the cannon rounds] and I observed four strikes after of the cockpit. I was unable to observe further results because I had one 109 on my tail and another positioning to attack.'[20]

The final recorded 'kills' by the Ta 152H occurred on 24 April, and again Willi Reschke was the victorious pilot. On this occasion his quarry were Soviet Yak-9s, which he judged 'hopelessly inferior to my Ta 152'.[21] He claimed two of the Russian fighters shot down near Berlin. The Ta 152H's final tally of 'kills' is believed to be seven, with several more probables.

Though it never got the opportunity to show what it could do at the altitudes for which it had been designed to operate, even as Nazi Germany was crumbling the Ta 152H did prove a formidable opponent for the Allies. Fortunately, only a handful entered operational service, and far too late to have any impact in the air war that had already long since been lost by the Luftwaffe.

Nachthöhenjägers

Besides the potential threat of US bombers like the B-29 attacking Germany by day, the Luftwaffe also had to contend with the very real problem of the RAF's fast, nimble Mosquitoes, operating both by day and night. From June 1942, Mosquito B.Mk IVs had been carrying out daring, pinpoint attacks on high-profile targets across the Reich.

The 'Mossie' incensed Goering. After three Mosquito B.Mk IVs of No 105 Sqn bombed the German state broadcasting station in Berlin on 31 January 1943, disrupting a national radio broadcast Goering was giving to mark the 10th anniversary of the Nazis coming to power, the humiliated Reichsmarschall famously exploded: 'It makes me furious when I see the Mosquito. I turn green and yellow with envy.'[22]

Determined to bring the Mosquito menace to an end, in March 1943 Goering ordered the formation of two dedicated anti-Mosquito fighter units, led by two of the Luftwaffe's most successful aces, to hunt the Mosquitoes flying PR sorties over the Reich by day. *Jagdgeschwader* 25 was based at Gardelegen and Berlin-Staaken, covering northern Germany and commanded by Knight's Cross holder Oberstleutnant Herbert Ihlefeld. Meanwhile, commanding *Jagdgeschwader* 50, which covered central and southern Germany from its base at Wiesbaden-Erbenheim, was Major Hermann Graf, another Knight's Cross recipient and the first pilot in the history of aerial warfare to achieve 200 'kills'. Both units became operational in July 1943, mostly equipped with the Bf 109G-5, with pressurised cockpit and the GM-1 power boost system.[23]

Despite boasting some of the most accomplished fighter pilots in the Luftwaffe, neither JG 25 nor JG 50 achieved much success against the Mosquito, scoring only a couple of confirmed 'kills'. By the end of the year both squadrons had been disbanded.

The Mosquito menace only grew worse in 1944 with Bomber Command's introduction of the B.Mk XVI. Developed in parallel with the PR.Mk XVI variant, this was a Mosquito Mk IX with two-stage Merlin 72/73 engines and a pressurised cabin, giving it a maximum ceiling of 42,000ft, and an enlarged, strengthened bomb bay, allowing it to carry the 4,000lb 'Cookie' bomb. The A & AEE test pilots reported that, 'The pressure cabin functions satisfactorily in all conditions of flight', and 'internal misting is confined to the single layer portions of the transparent parts of the cabin; the double layer portions remain clear up to 35,000ft'. One of the few criticisms of the Mk XVI was that 'during taxying and at low altitude the cabin was uncomfortably warm'.[24]

The first B.Mk XVI was completed in October 1943 and began entering service in early 1944, eight squadrons eventually being equipped with the type. No 692 Squadron carried out the first operational sortie with 'Cookie' bombs – a raid on Duisberg – on the night of 5/6 March 1944. Navigational aids like Oboe and Gee-H ensured a fair degree of bombing accuracy at high level was achieved. Indeed, in November 1944 the AOC of the RAF's Pathfinder Force, Air Vice Marshal Bennett, congratulated the Mosquito B.Mk XVI-equipped No 571 Squadron on having 'reached a standard of accuracy of a high order'.[25]

The regular harassment raids by 'Cookie'–carrying Mosquitoes further gnawed away at the morale of the Germans, as Goebbels privately admitted. 'The air terror which rages uninterruptedly over German home territory makes people thoroughly despondent,' he wrote in a diary entry after a Mosquito raid, and fumed that the bomber was 'almost impossible to shoot down'.[26]

Partly in response to these Mosquito raids, the RLM ordered the development of several high-altitude night-fighter (*nachthöhenjäger*) projects during the second half of the war.

Widely regarded as the most effective German night-fighter of the Second World War, the Heinkel He 219 was an obvious choice for adaptation to meet this requirement. Entering production in early 1943, only a relatively small number of He 219s were produced (less than 300), partly due to Milch's opposition to the type. But from its service debut in mid-1943 until the end of the war, the He 219 proved a particularly deadly opponent for RAF bomber crews. It even enjoyed some success against the pesky Mosquitoes, reportedly shooting down six of them in its first ten days of operations in June 1943.

The high-altitude version of the He 219 was the B-2 model. This was to feature a pressurised cockpit, extended wings and be powered by the Jumo 222, though ongoing development troubles with the 222 unit meant that the DB 603 had to be substituted. Several test machines were produced but the model didn't enter production. Another proposed high-altitude version was the He 419, with a projected service ceiling in the region of 45,000ft, but it's unclear if any were in fact built.

Germany's other *nachthöhenjäger* project was the 'J' model of the Ju 388. Derived from the Ju 188, and also developed into bomber and reconnaissance variants – the 'K' and 'L' model, respectively – the 'J' nightfighter version would feature heavy armament, consisting of a mix of MG 15 7.92mm machine guns and Mk 108 30mm cannon, and the FuG 218 'Neptun' radar. Shortages of the planned Jumo 213 engine meant that the test machines would be fitted with the BMW 801TJ supercharged engine. A ceiling of 38,000ft was anticipated.

In July 1944 an operational evaluation unit, *Erprobungskommando* 388 (or Edko 388), had been formed at Rechlin for intensive testing, initially equipped with five Ju 388 prototypes. With the Luftwaffe's overriding priority now the air defence of Germany, interest in the bomber and reconnaissance versions dissipated and in October Edko 388 was instructed to concentrate solely on testing of the Ju 388J night-fighter model, with decorated night-fighter ace Hauptmann Kurt Bonow appointed to command the unit. However, the performance of the Ju 388J failed to live up to expectations. The highest altitude Bonow reached while test flying the Ju 388 was 33,560ft, and he found that even at this height the flight characteristics 'were no longer satisfactory'.[27]

The poor results of the test flights led to the cancellation of plans to start production of the Ju 388J in January 1945, and the following month Edko 388 was disbanded. A few of the Ju 388Js already built were also rumoured to have been used in the last months of the war as launch platforms in tests of the Ruhrstahl X-4 air-to-air missile.[28]

Chapter Ten

Japan versus the Superforts

As with the Germans in Europe in the first two years of the war, much of the success of Japan's military campaigns in the early stages of the Pacific War was due in no small measure to effective photo-reconnaissance carried out by high-flying spy planes. The most important PR aircraft operated by the Japanese during the Second World War was undoubtedly the Ki-46.

The Mitsubishi Ki-46 resulted from a specification issued in December 1937 by the *Koku Hombu* (Army Air Headquarters) for a long-range reconnaissance aircraft which should have an endurance of six hours and be capable of flying at high altitude, to replace the Ki-15 in JAAF service. The Mitsubishi design team, led by Tomio Kuba, produced an elegant design, powered by two Ha-26 engines, with the prototype making its maiden flight in November 1939 from Mitsubishi's factory near Nagoya. As this was unable to meet the performance requirements demanded by the JAAF, a Mark II version was produced, which replaced the engines with Ha-102 radials fitted with a two-speed supercharger.

First taking to the air in March 1941, the Mk II had a top speed of 375 mph and could reach 36,000ft, though it lacked a pressurised cockpit. Satisfied with its improved performance, the JAAF ordered the Ki-46 II into production, with the first examples reaching frontline squadrons in July. With plans for the invasions of the European colonial possessions in Asia by then well advanced, the entry into service of this excellent reconnaissance asset could not have been more timely. In October 1941, Ki-46s of the 51st Independent *Chutai*, flying from their base at Kompong Trach in Cambodia, carried out photo-reconnaissance of British defences in Malaya prior to the Japanese invasion of the colony in December. The Philippines, Burma and the Dutch East Indies were also extensively photographed in advance of the Japanese conquest of these territories. The Ki-46's qualities were also recognised by the JNAF, who operated small numbers of the type.

Initially, the crews of the Ki-46 – given the codename 'Dinah' by the Allies – went about their business with little interference from US, Dutch, and British and Commonwealth forces in the Far East, which were equipped with mostly obsolescent fighters incapable of reaching the Ki-46's operating altitudes, like the Brewster Buffalo and Curtiss P-40. Gradually, however, the situation began to change, as more modern equipment reached the Pacific theatre. In early 1943 No 1 Fighter Wing, comprising No 54 (RAF), 452 (RAAF) and 457 (RAAF) Sqns arrived in Australia with the first Spitfires (Mk Vs) to defend Darwin from the regular bombing raids being mounted on the northern Australian harbour by the Japanese. These raids were invariably preceded by 'Dinah' aircraft, flying recce sorties from their bases on Timor in the Dutch East Indies.

After a bumpy start by pilots more used to the very different tactics being employed by the Germans in Europe and North Africa, the new arrivals eventually got the measure of their new foe. The first 'Dinah' was shot down by a pair of Spitfires on 7 March 1943, Flight Lieutenant MacLean and Flight Sergeant McDowell of No 457 Sqn sharing the kill. 'Both pilots delivered the attacks at close range upon the enemy reconnaissance aircraft "Dinah" when it was heading for home over the sea about 15 miles from Darwin. There was no return fire from the aircraft, which plunged, burning fiercely, into the sea,' stated the Squadron's Operations Record Book.[1]

By the end of 1943 'Dinah' crews were also encountering Spitfires over India, Mk Vs of No 607 and 615 Sqn having been despatched to Alipore in September to protect Indian airspace from the high-flying Japanese spy planes. Three Ki-46s were shot down by Spitfires of 615 Sqn during November. After another 'Dinah' was brought down by the Squadron's pilots on 15 January 1944, 615's ORB commented that their 'bag' of Dinahs 'grows nearly as often as they appear.'[2]

Anticipating the arrival of more capable enemy fighters, in July 1942 the *Koku Hombu* had instructed Mitsubishi to deliver an improved Ki-46, with greater speed and ceiling. By omitting defensive armament, redesigning the nose so that it formed a perfectly streamlined teardrop shape and installing new fuel-injected Ha-112 engines, the Ki-46 III could reach 404 mph and had a slightly improved ceiling. So impressed was the JAAF with this new mark that work on the Ki-46's intended replacement, the Tachikawa Ki-70, was suspended.

Frontline squadrons began receiving the Ki-46 III during 1943, but ever strengthening Allied fighter opposition throughout the Pacific theatre made it increasingly difficult for the 'Dinah' to penetrate enemy airspace, and what had been a virtually untouchable aircraft in 1942 became cannon fodder for the Allies by 1945.

The Dinah's lack of a pressurised cabin restricted the maximum altitude at which its crews could safely operate. Even before the outbreak of hostilities with the Western powers, this weakness was recognised by the Japanese, and in 1939 the Tachikawa company had begun work on a long-range PR aircraft, designed from the outset to be equipped with a pressure cabin, which could reach 40,000ft.

Tachikawa had been at the forefront of Japanese research into aircraft pressurisation. In the late 1930s the company had developed a pressure cabin for the Army's Type LO transport aircraft (given the codename 'Thelma' by the Allies). Ironically, the Type LO was based on the American Lockheed Model 14 Super Electra airliner, almost 200 of which were built under licence by Tachikawa and Kawasaki prior to the outbreak of hostilities with the United States. A single research aircraft fitted with the new pressure cabin, designated the Tachikawa SS-1 and powered by twin Mitsubishi Ha-102 engines, was constructed.

Using the knowledge gained from the SS-1 programme, Tachikawa produced the Ki-74 long-range PR aircraft. A twin-engine machine with a wingspan of 61ft and a range of 4,970 miles, the first two prototypes were powered by Ha-112 engines with turbo-superchargers. Development was protracted, however, and it wasn't until March 1944 that the first flight took place, five years after the project had been initiated. Reliability issues with the Ha-112 unit led to its substitution with the more dependable Ha-104 engine on the subsequent pre-production machines, which gave it a maximum speed of 354 mph and a ceiling of 39,370ft. When the Allies learnt of the Ki-74's existence, it was assigned the reporting name 'Pat', in the mistaken belief that the type was a heavy fighter. After it became clear the Ki-74 was intended for reconnaissance, the name was changed to 'Patsy'.[3] Only sixteen were built, none of which are believed to have seen operational service.

Allied reconnaissance in the Far East

With the war in Europe and North Africa consuming the bulk of the RAF's resources in the first half of the war, precious little could be spared for the Far East. This was particularly so in the case of photo-reconnaissance assets. When the Japanese launched their invasions of Britain's colonial possessions in Asia in December 1941, the only PR aircraft available to the RAF in the Far East were some Lockheed Hudsons and Bristol Blenheims.

In late 1942 the first PR Spitfires arrived in the Far East, a pair of PR.Mk IVs which carried out sorties over Burma from India. Originally designated the PR.Mk I Type D, the PR.Mk IV was a modified version of the Mk V fighter, with enlarged wing tanks, each containing 66 gallons, giving it a maximum range of just over 1,800 miles. No 681 Squadron, based at Dum Dum in India and later at Alipore, operated the type from January 1943 until December 1944. Once they could be spared from the European theatre, additional PR Spitfires, including some Mk XIs, were sent to India. Joining the Spitfires at Dum Dum and Alipore from late 1943 were pressurised Mosquito

PR.Mk XVIs of No 684 Squadron, to provide long-range coverage of Burma. In June 1945 a detachment was sent to the Cocos Islands, taking with them several of the new Mosquito PR.Mk 34s. From there, they carried out a total of thirty-eight PR sorties, mainly covering Sumatra and Malaya. The fastest of all marks of Mosquito, the PR.Mk 34 had a top speed of 422 mph, a maximum range of 3,340 miles and could reach 43,000ft.

The mainstay of USAAF reconnaissance in the Pacific was the Lockheed F-5, the PR variant of the P-38 Lightning fighter. This had a range of 1,300 miles and a ceiling of over 40,000ft. But given the vast distances involved in this theatre of operations, there was a need for an extremely long-range, strategic PR platform, which could reach the Japanese home islands from Allied-held airfields in China. One of the key proponents of such a machine was Colonel Elliot Roosevelt, son of the US President, who served as a reconnaissance pilot in the war and was only too aware of the limitations of the F-5.

In 1943 the USAAF issued a demanding specification for a purpose-built, strategic reconnaissance aircraft, with a range of 4,500 miles, a service ceiling of 45,000ft and a maximum speed of 400 mph. Republic Aviation responded with the XF-12 'Rainbow'. An extremely sleek, aerodynamic design, the XF-12 was fitted with a pressure cabin in its cigar-shaped fuselage and four Pratt & Whitney Wasp Major engines. Two prototypes were ordered, though the first of these wasn't ready for flight testing until after the war against Japan had concluded. It made its maiden flight on 4 February 1946, during which test pilot Lowery L. Brabham successfully reached the specified height of 45,000ft. But the XF-12 was just too late on the scene and the project was eventually cancelled.

Another contender to fill the USAAF's requirement for a long-range, high-altitude PR machine was the controversial Hughes XF-11. A twin-engine aircraft, this resembled an enlarged P-38 Lightning. One hundred were ordered in 1943, allegedly after Howard Hughes, chairman of the Hughes Aircraft Company, had influenced the USAAF's procurement decision, though endless development problems ensured it would never enter operational service. Only two were built.

Enter the 'Superfort'

Fortunately, the failure of these projects to enter production was not as serious as it might have been, for the Americans had another aircraft which, though not originally intended for the role, would prove well-suited to long-range, high-altitude photo-reconnaissance work – the B-29 Superfortress.

Undoubtedly the most important and technically advanced bomber programme of the Second World War, the Boeing B-29 was conceived in 1938 as a replacement for the same company's B-17 Flying Fortress. The B-29 would have a colossal range of 5,830 miles, a service ceiling of 33,600ft, an awesome maximum bombload of 20,000lbs, and would bristle with four pairs of .50 calibre machine guns in remotely operated turrets and a fifth, manned tail turret containing twin .50s and a single 20mm cannon. The B-29's most impressive technical achievement, however, was its pressurised compartments in the cockpit and rear fuselage, linked by an access tunnel running the length of the fuselage, which allowed its crew to function on the long missions at 30,000ft.

Although the programme had no shortage of detractors, both within Congress and the US War Department, the outbreak of war in Europe and growing Japanese aggression in Asia ensured the programme would overcome all obstacles to enter service. Indeed, the importance attached to the long-range, high-altitude heavy bomber was such that a second project, the Consolidated B-32 Dominator, was concurrently set in train as a contingency, in the event that technical problems delayed or even scuppered the B-29.[4]

In 1941 the B-29 was given the name Superfortress, and the prototype (serial number 41-002) first took to the air on 21 September 1942, from Boeing Field in Seattle, Washington, with the company's Director of Flight Research Edmund T. Allen at the controls. Full production went ahead from 1943, shared between several aircraft manufacturers, with much of the final assembly work carried out at Boeing's massive new factory in Wichita, Kansas. Such was the pressing demand for the B-29 in the war against Japan that the Superfortress was rushed into frontline service before all the technical issues could be resolved, the most alarming of which being a tendency for the Wright R-3350 Duplex Cyclone engines to catch fire. Eventually, however, most of the problems were overcome and the B-29 went on to become a war-winning weapon.

In April 1944 more than a hundred of the early production models, the B-29BW and B-29A, were selected for conversion to PR aircraft, the work being carried out by the Continental Air Lines Denver Modification Center. The modifications included sealing the bomb bay and installing a camera fit comprising three K-17Bs, two K-22s and a single K-18 camera, in the rear pressurised fuselage section. The powerful defensive armament was retained. This PR variant of the B-29 was named the F-13 and F-13A.

The unit chosen to operate the F-13 in the Pacific was the 3rd Photographic Reconnaissance Squadron, under the command of Lieutenant Colonel Patrick McCarthy. The first F-13s of the 3rd PRS arrived on the island of Saipan, 1,500 miles south of Japan, on 30 October 1944, their task being to provide the USAAF's 21st Bomber Command with pre and post-strike imagery of targets in Japan. On 1 November the unit carried out its first reconnaissance mission over the Japanese home islands, 'Tokyo Rose' (as it would later be named), flown by Captain Ralph Streakley, photographing industrial targets in and around Tokyo from a height of around 32,000ft. Among the Japanese fighters scrambled to intercept were Nakajima Ki-44 'Tojos' of the JAAF's 47th *Sentai*, flying out of Narimasu airfield.

The 'Tojo' was felt suitable for home defence duties as it possessed the fastest rate of climb of all the JAAF's fighters and had a heavy armament (including, in some examples, a 40mm cannon). On the downside, when laden with fuel and ammunition it became almost uncontrollable at very high altitudes. Several of the Ki-44s struggled up to 30,000ft and, while still below the F-13, fired a few bursts in desperation before their pilots lost control and had to descend to lower altitude. After a flight lasting fourteen hours, during which the crew took over 700 photographs, 'Tokyo Rose' landed safely back at Saipan. This sortie, for which Captain Streakley was awarded the DFC and his crew the Air Medal, marked the first time an Allied aircraft had flown over Tokyo since the B-25s of the famous 'Doolittle Raid' in April 1942.

A second F-13 sortie was flown over Tokyo six days later. On this occasion, over 100 fighters were scrambled, but again none were able to reach the F-13's height. One of the 3rd PRS's pilots, Lieutenant Fred Savage, later said: 'We would fly our F-13A at about 30,000ft during photo missions because Japanese fighter aircraft could not reach us.'[5] But not all F-13 missions were flown at high-altitude. Cloud cover over some targets often forced F-13 crews to descend through the cloud base to lower altitude to take their photographs, which of course put them at greater risk from flak and fighter defences.

As more F-13s arrived from the US, by the end of 1944 the squadron was carrying out an average of thirty sorties per month, photographing the major industrial centres of Japan. F-13s also acted as decoys, single examples deploying 'window' ('chaff' in USAAF parlance) to create fake bomber streams on Japanese radar so as to draw away enemy fighters from actual B-29 bomber formations heading for their targets in Japan.

Bombing Japan

The F-13 PR flights were not the first encounters Japanese fighter pilots had had with the mighty Superfortress. In April 1944 the first B-29 bombers of the 58th Bombardment Wing of the 20th Bomber Command arrived at forward airfields in Chengdu in southern China, after staging through bases in northeast India. The Chinese airfields were incredibly austere, and the logistics effort required to sustain the B-29 force was immense, with all the Wing's supplies having to be transported by air over the Himalayas (known to the crews as 'the Hump') from Allied bases in India, 1,200 miles away.

The first clash between Japanese fighters and the new bomber occurred on 26 April 1944, when Ki-43 'Oscars' of the 64th and 204th *Sentais* attacked a single B-29, flown by Major Charles Hansen at 16,000ft near the Chinese-Indian border, though the Ki-43's light armament was insufficient to do any real damage to the Superfortress. On 5 June the 58th Bombardment Wing carried out its first raid, against railway yards at Bangkok, Thailand. Five bombers were lost on this mission, none to enemy action. Ten days later the 58th BW mounted its first raid against Japan itself, sixty-eight Superfortresses – each carrying a reduced bombload of 4,000lbs – raiding the Imperial Steel and Iron Works in Yawata in the southern Japanese island of Kyushu. Twin-engine Kawasaki Ki-45 *Toryu* ('Dragon Slayer') night-fighters of the 4th *Sentai* at Ozuki airfield were scrambled to intercept.

Seeing the B-29 for the first time was an intimidating experience for the Japanese airmen. Ki-45 pilot Lieutenant Isamu Kashiide recalled that when he first encountered the bomber he was 'astounded' by its sheer size.[6] Heavy cloud cover prevented accurate bombing and little damage was done to the steelworks. Although the pilots of the 4th *Sentai* pilots claimed a total of seven B-29s shot down, in fact only a single bomber was lost to enemy action on that day.

It wasn't until November 1944 that the strategic bombing campaign against Japan really got into its stride, when the B-29s of the newly formed 21st Bomber Command under Brigadier General Haywood 'Possum' Hansell began operating from bases in the Marianas Islands, captured by US forces a few months earlier. The first raid on Tokyo was on 24 November 1944, over 100 B-29s of the 497th Bomber Group taking off from Saipan to attack the Musashino aircraft engine factory and nearby docks. Anticipating raids by the B-29s on Tokyo, Japan's fighter defences had by this time been strengthened, with Ki-44s, Ki-46s and Navy J2M3 *Raiden* fighters among those scrambled to intercept when radar plotted the inbound raid. Though B-29 losses were light, with only one confirmed to have been shot down by the defending fighters, the Americans failed to destroy the Musashino plant.

These early encounters with the B-29 had highlighted two critical weaknesses in the interceptors the Japanese squadrons were equipped with: their armament lacked sufficiently heavy firepower to bring down the giant bomber, and they struggled to reach the 30,000ft operating altitude of the Superfortress. One solution was to form specialised aerial ramming units within each *Sentai*. Known as *Shinten Seiku Tai* (Air Superiority Company), these comprised between four and eight fighters adapted for high-altitude ramming by the removal of armament, armour and all other equipment not absolutely essential for their task to improve the ceiling of their fighters. The Japanese refined their ramming tactics and soon found that head-on collisions into the cabin of the B-29, known as *Tai-Atari* (literally, 'body-crashing'), produced the most effective results. *Tai-Atari* attacks almost always resulted in the deaths of both the Japanese pilot and American flight crew.

But ramming attacks were wasteful of both men and machines. So efforts were also made to improve the ceiling and high-altitude performance of Japan's fighters. However, a shortage of the alloys necessary for the manufacture of turbo-superchargers were to seriously impede this effort.

Among the types modified as high-altitude anti-B-29 interceptors was the Ki-46 'Dinah' reconnaissance aircraft. With a ceiling of 40,000ft when filled with 95 octane fuel, and armed with two Ho-5 20mm cannon in the nose and a single Ho-204 37mm cannon in a *Schräge Musik* arrangement, it was felt that the 'Dinah' would be well-suited to tackling the Superfortress. But this version, the Ki-46 III *Kai* (meaning 'modified'), took around twenty-five minutes to reach 30,000ft. Given that Japanese radar could only give thirty minutes maximum advance warning of an incoming raid, this gave the defending pilot very little time to position himself for an attack. The Ki-46 III *Kai* also proved difficult to control at or near its maximum altitude. Some examples, stripped of armament, were used for high-altitude patrols to augment the Japanese radar network by visually detecting approaching B-29 formations. A dedicated interceptor variant, the Ki-46 IV, fitted with Ha-112 turbocharged engines, was also developed, but only four prototypes were built.

Modifications were also made to the Ki-44, which included enlarging the engine lubricant pipe to increase the flow of oil, which helped prevent a loss of power in the thin air at high altitude. The JNAF's standard fighter, the Mitsubishi A6M 'Zero', was another to undergo modifications to improve its ceiling. Originally designed to defend ships of the Japanese

Imperial Fleet from torpedo-bombers and dive-bombers carrying out low-level attacks, the Zero was never intended to fight at very high altitudes. But as the most widely produced Japanese fighter of the war, inevitably the Zero was pressed into service to defend the homeland against the Superfortress.

Efforts were made to install a Sakae turbo-supercharged engine in the A6M2 airframe. Two prototypes were built, designated the A6M4, and underwent flight testing in 1943 at the Yokosuka Arsenal, but the engines had a tendency to catch fire. While the later A6M5 model could reach 38,000ft, the slow rate of climb (taking thirty minutes to reach its maximum altitude) greatly restricted its usefulness as a B-29 destroyer. Nor did Mitsubishi have any better luck with a high-altitude version of their J2M *Raiden* fighter, the Model 33, which despite fitting a supercharger to its engine also struggled to reach the B-29's height.

Another type modified for high-altitude interception was Kawasaki's Ki-102 (Allied codename 'Randy'). A twin-engine fighter with a two-man crew, this was intended to replace the company's successful Ki-45. Entering service in small numbers in 1945, the Ki-102's heavy armament, good rate of climb and impressive endurance convinced the IJA it would provide the basis for an effective high-altitude bomber destroyer. Renamed the Ki-108, four examples were rebuilt with pressure cabins, accommodating a pilot only, but the Ki-108 failed to reach production status.

One of the more successful attempts to modify an existing fighter as a high-altitude interceptor was the Kawasaki Ki-100 *Goshikisen* (Type 5 fighter). By taking the airframe of a Ki-61 *Hien* (Allied codename 'Tony') and substituting its Ha-140

V-12 inline engine (a licence-built version of the Daimler-Benz DB 605) with a Mitsubishi Ha-112 radial, the Kawasaki engineers produced what was widely regarded as one of the finest Japanese fighters of the war. A total of 275 Ki-100s were produced and the type made its combat debut on 9 March 1945. While proving reasonably effective at intercepting the B-29, it was felt that the high-altitude performance could be further improved. This led to the final variant, the Ki-100 II, with a turbocharged water-methanol injected engine, though only three were completed by the end of the war, none of which saw operational service.

New fighters

Besides adapting existing fighters, like the British and the Germans, the Japanese also put great effort into producing a dedicated interceptor designed from the outset for high-altitude operations. A specification for such a machine was issued by the *Koku Hombu* in 1942, with Nakajima and Tachikawa selected to compete for the contract.

Nakajima's offering was the Ki-87. Designed by a team led by Kunihiro Aoki, it was a large fighter, bearing a resemblance to the US P-47 Thunderbolt, which was powered by an Ha-44 air-cooled radial engine and equipped with a turbo-supercharger mounted on the starboard side of the fuselage. Armament consisted of two Ho-5 20mm and two Ho-155 30mm cannon in the wings. A pressurised cockpit was planned, to allow the Ki-87 to reach its intended ceiling of 42,175ft, and considerable armour plating to protect the pilot from the B-29's heavy defensive fire was also provided.

Three prototypes were ordered, with completion due by January 1945, while seven pre-production aircraft were to be delivered by April 1945. Technical problems with the turbo-supercharger and complicated landing gear assembly caused this schedule to slip, and in the event only one prototype (lacking the pressurised cockpit) was completed, in February 1945. A total of five test flights were carried out with this aircraft, beginning in April, but its performance could not be properly assessed as fears over the reliability of the electrical system powering the landing gear meant that it flew with the undercarriage in the fixed position. After the war this aircraft was captured by US forces at Chofu air base near Tokyo, who, impressed by its size, christened it 'Big Boy'.[7] The second and third prototypes were found partially complete.

While the Ki-87 was undergoing its flight tests, preliminary development work had already begun on an improved version, the Ki-87 II. The main planned differences were the substitution of the Ha-44 with an Ha-219 engine, increasing the power to 3,000 hp, and the repositioning of the turbo-supercharger to the rear of the fuselage. However, this version progressed no further than the drawing board before the Japanese surrender.

In contrast to the Nakajima Ki-87, Tachikawa's proposal to meet the *Koku Hombu*'s high-altitude interceptor requirement was altogether more radical. The Ki-94, designed by a team under Tatsuo Hasegawa, featured a twin-boom layout like the P-38 Lightning and would be powered by two Mitsubishi Ha-211 air-cooled, radial engines in a 'push-pull' arrangement – one positioned in front of, the other behind, the cockpit. Armament would consist of two Ho-155 30mm and two Ho-204 37mm cannon. A wooden mock-up was built, but when this was presented to officials of the *Koku Hombu* in October 1943 for evaluation, it was felt the design was just too radical and Tachikawa's estimated performance figures – a top speed of 485 mph and maximum ceiling of 45,900ft – unachievable. Therefore, the Ki-94 proposal was rejected.

Undeterred, Hasegawa and his team went back to the drawing board and came up with an entirely new design to meet the specification. Learning from past mistakes, Hasegawa played it safe with a design for a much more conventional, single engine fighter, the Ki-94 II, which was very similar in appearance to the Nakajima Ki-87. This approach proved successful, with the *Koku Hombu* placing an order for three prototypes – the first of which was to be ready to fly by 20 July 1945 – followed by eighteen pre-production examples.

In the event, only one prototype was completed by war's end, fitted with an Ha-44 radial engine and turbo-supercharger. Whether or not the Ki-94 II would have been capable of achieving its estimated ceiling of 46,750ft would never be known, however, as the Japanese surrender came three days before its first flight was scheduled to take place.

As the war situation deteriorated for Japan during 1945, and with the development of their own projects progressing at a slow pace, the Japanese turned to their German ally for help in providing a quick solution to their pressing need for a high-altitude interceptor. As the only specialised German single engine, high-altitude fighter to enter production, and having been originally conceived to tackle the B-29 when there were fears of its deployment against Germany, the Focke-Wulf Ta 152H was the obvious choice. Thus, in April 1945 Japan bought the plans and rights to manufacture the Ta 152 under licence. However, it is not known if the plans actually reached Japan. If they did, no evidence appears to exist that the Japanese had begun work on their own version of Focke-Wulf's high-flyer before the war ended.

And so the JAAF and JNAF had to struggle on with the largely inadequate fighters already in service. Difficulties in flying at high altitude over Japan were not confined to the defending fighter pilots, however. The B-29 crews were experiencing problems of their own while conducting operations at 30,000ft. Cloud cover and the powerful jet stream that buffeted the bombers made accurate bombing all but impossible. An official US report compiled in 1946 which assessed the American strategic bombing offensive against Japan concluded that, during the initial phase of the campaign, less than 10 per cent of the bombs dropped hit their targets.[8]

A new approach was clearly needed. On 20 January 1945, Brigadier General Hansell was replaced as commander of 21st Bomber Command by General Curtis E. LeMay. With the change in leadership came a change of strategy. Hansell's policy of high-altitude precision attacks against specific military and industrial targets was largely abandoned in favour of area bombing at medium altitude. While this at first led to increased losses among the B-29 force, LeMay's controversial new tactics successfully laid waste to Japan's major cities.

From April 1945 Japan's increasingly hard-pressed fighter force not only had to deal with the heavy defensive fire of the B-29s, but also long-range P-47N Thunderbolt and P-51D Mustang fighters, based on Iwo Jima and, later, Okinawa, which were now escorting the bombers to their targets. By the summer, critical shortages of fuel and trained pilots reduced to negligible levels the fighter opposition the JAAF and JNAF could muster against the B-29s. In August, the B-29 delivered the fatal blows to Japan with the dropping of the atomic bombs on Hiroshima and Nagasaki.

A Japanese Superfortress

Like the Germans, during the pre-war years the Japanese had neglected the development of long-range, strategic heavy bombers in favour of tactical, twin-engine medium bombers and single-engine dive bombers, designed to support the Army and the Navy. This left Japan with no means to strike at the Continental United States, or targets deep within the Soviet Union.

This weakness had, in fact, been identified as far back as 1938, when the IJN instructed Nakajima to produce a design for a long-range heavy bomber. Nakajima used as the basis for its new bomber project the prototype of the Douglas DC-4E pressurised airliner it had acquired in 1939, disguising Japanese military involvement in the purchase by using a front company – the Mitsui Trading Co.[9]

The heavily re-engineered and redesigned DC-4E eventually emerged as the Nakajima G5N1 *Shinzan* (meaning 'Mountain Recess'). In April 1941 the prototype made its maiden flight, but like the DC-4E it was overweight and complex, with the four NK7A Mamoru engines proving to be both unreliable and underpowered. To remedy the situation, the next two prototypes were completed with Mitsubishi Kasei 12 engines, but this failed to cure the lack of power. Known to the Allies by the codename 'Liz', six *Shinzans* were built in all, several of which were used as transports but none in their intended bombing role.

With the demise of the G5N1 *Shinzan* project, in September 1943 the Imperial Japanese Navy issued a revised specification to Nakajima for a four-engine heavy bomber, with a range of 4,600 miles and maximum bombload of 8,800lbs. From this emerged the Nakajima G8N1 *Renzan* ('Mountain Range'), known to the Allies as 'Rita'. The first prototype was completed in October 1944 and performed its maiden flight on the 23rd of that month. With its performance deemed to be satisfactory, three more prototypes were ordered, with the IJN aiming for delivery of sixteen pre-production and forty-eight production aircraft by September 1945. Only four, however, were completed by the end of the war.[10] In June 1945, with the air defence of the home islands now the priority and critical shortages of aluminium severely curtailing aircraft production, the Navy ordered Nakajima to halt work on the *Renzan* and focus instead on fighters.

Meanwhile, the JAAF was pursuing its own plans for a heavy bomber with a capability to attack the United States. One idea was to revive the Tachikawa Ki-74, originally conceived as a long-range reconnaissance aircraft, and adapt it for bombing. Although the Ki-74 was a twin-engine aircraft and could carry only a relatively modest bombload of 2,200lbs, it was capable of reaching a height of 39,370ft.

In September 1942 the *Koku Hombu* ordered three prototypes of the Ki-74 bomber variant, the first of these being ready for flight testing in March 1944. This example featured a pressurised cockpit mounted atop the fuselage and offset to port, two Mitsubishi Ha-211 engines and, as it would rely chiefly on its height for protection, light defensive armament comprising a single, remote-controlled Ho-103 12.7mm machine gun housed in a tail barbette. Fifteen more Ki-74s were completed, most swapping the Ha-211s – which testing with the first prototype had revealed were unreliable – with Mitsubishi Ha-104 engines.

Among the missions envisaged for the Ki-74 were one-way bombing sorties against the United States, attacks on the B-29 bases in Saipan, and non-stop transport flights from Japanese-held territory to Germany. But the protracted flight testing phase ensured none of these ambitious plans would be realised. Preliminary work had also commenced on a revised bomber version, the Ki-74 II, which would feature a redesigned, more compact pressure cabin and be capable of carrying twice the bombload of the Mark I model. The Ki-74 II never made it to the construction stage.

It was recognised by the JAAF that if they were to strike at the United States, a four-engine bomber would be required. The initial plan to acquire such a machine was to have Nakajima develop another version of their G5N1 *Shinzan*. The Nakajima Ki-68 would have substituted the troublesome NK7A powerplants with Mitsubishi Ha-101 engines. But the cancellation of the *Shinzan* project in 1943 doomed this plan, along with another for Kawanishi to build a version powered by four Mitsubishi Ha-111M engines, the Ki-85, which only advanced to the stage of a wooden mock-up being built.

Kawasaki then took on the challenge. In the summer of 1943 design work began on the Ki-91. At almost 108ft long and with a wingspan of 156ft, this would be slightly larger even than the B-29 Superfortress. Power would come from four Mitsubishi Ha-214 supercharged engines, giving a top speed of 360 mph and ceiling of 44,219ft, which would necessitate the installation of a pressure cabin for its eight-man crew. A bombload of 8,800lbs could be carried over a range of 6,200 miles. The Ki-91 would also share with the B-29 a heavy defensive armament, amounting to no fewer than twelve 20mm cannon, housed in nose, dorsal, ventral and tail turrets.

Impressed by a full-scale wooden mock-up presented for inspection in May 1944, the IJA gave the go-ahead for a prototype to be built. If all went well, the JAAF planned to use their bomber to attack the United States from the Kurile Islands, a distance of some 4,200 miles. In February 1945, with the prototype almost two-thirds complete, the project suffered a fatal blow when the Kawasaki factory in Gifu Prefecture was bombed by B-29s, destroying much of the plant. Days later the Ki-91 was cancelled.

The most ambitious Japanese long-range heavy bomber project of the war was Nakajima's Fugaku.[11] The driving force behind the Fugaku ('Mount Fuji') was the company's chairman Chikuhei Nakajima, who developed a plan for a transpacific bomber to attack the United States, known as Project Z, on his own initiative after his proposal was rejected by the IJA and IJN when he first submitted it.

The vast distances the bomber would have to cover while carrying a worthwhile bombload demanded a very large aircraft, and the design Nakajima's team came up with was a true giant – almost 131ft long, with a wingspan of 206ft and powered by six engines. Maximum bombload would be a phenomenal 44,000lbs (more than double that of a B-29). With a range of over 10,000 miles, the aircraft would be capable of making a round bombing trip from Japan to the west coast of the United States. The intended defensive armament would be quite light, amounting to four Type 99 20mm cannon, as the Fugaku would rely on its great altitude – projected ceiling was 49,200ft – for protection from fighter interception.

By the time the basic design was set and presented to Army and Navy officials again in April 1943, the demand for some means to attack America was greater and the Fugaku concept was looked upon more favourably. Nakajima was therefore instructed to further develop the design, while in autumn of that year construction began on a new factory at Mitaka, Tokyo, to build the bomber. However, the IJA doubted the feasibility of the project and dropped out. The Ministry of Munitions shared their doubts and secretly ordered Kawanishi to design a rival bomber, on a more modest scale. Their offering, the TB, would be considerably smaller and powered by only four engines. Maximum bombload and ceiling would also be more realistic, at 12,000lbs and 41,665ft, respectively.

Neither the Fugaku nor the TB were destined to make it any further than the drawing board, both projects being scrapped in 1944 as Japan's priorities and dwindling resources switched to air defence of the homeland.

Chapter Eleven

Hitler's Retaliation Bombers

During 1943 the combined Allied bombing offensive against Germany, with the US Eighth Air Force attacking by day and RAF Bomber Command by night, was wreaking enormous destruction on Hitler's Reich. In the course of that year the British and Americans dropped a total of over 200,000 tons of bombs on Germany, killing tens of thousands of civilians (many of them in the firestorm that engulfed the city of Hamburg in July). Infuriated by this punishing aerial offensive, Hitler demanded reprisal attacks on Britain. German industry was already hard at work developing so-called *vergeltung* ('retaliation') weapons in the form of the V1 'doodlebug' missile and V2 ballistic rocket, but it would be some time before these revolutionary weapons would reach operational status. In the meantime, Hitler ordered the commencement of a third branch of *vergeltung* weapon development – pressurised high-altitude bombers.

As we have seen, the Luftwaffe had already mounted a high-altitude bombing campaign against the UK on a very modest scale using the Ju 86R in the late summer of 1942, with some success. But Hitler envisaged something much more ambitious: a new generation of bombers, capable of carrying a much greater bombload than the Ju 86R, to pound British cities from an altitude of 45,000ft. In March 1943 he ordered Milch 'to build high altitude and fast bombers and put them first on the production line'. Milch argued that fighters for home defence should instead take priority,[1] but Hitler was adamant that the Luftwaffe must take the offensive. Two months later he summoned Germany's leading aircraft designers to a meeting at his private residence, the Berghof in Obersalzberg, to discuss the state of the country's aviation industry and future projects, without Goering, Milch or any other Luftwaffe representatives being present.

Among those called in to speak with Hitler was Ernst Heinkel. He and the Führer discussed the company's four-engine heavy bomber, the He 177, which was suffering no end of technical problems. The conversation then turned to the subject of high-altitude bombing of Britain. 'Ultimately he began to develop a theme which was obviously a great favourite,' Heinkel recalled in his autobiography. 'He wanted forty or fifty planes which could fly over England at 45,000ft, out of reach of enemy fighters, and appear in shifts over London to bomb it day and night. "Such continuous bombing attacks," he said, "would bring life there to a standstill." He felt a desperate need to hit back in some way at England.'[2]

Heinkel was already well aware of the Nazi high command's desperation for such a machine. He had been among the German aircraft industrialists and senior RLM officials present at a conference convened by an angry Goering at Karinhall on 18 March 1943, when the same topic had been raised by the Reichsmarschall as he subjected them all to a tirade over their failure to provide the Luftwaffe with suitable new bomber types:

You remember, gentlemen, that I spoke of the high-altitude bomber and the high-speed bomber even before the war. At that time I offered tax-free million mark awards to designers and others who could produce something serviceable. Throughout the war I have constantly reminded them that high-altitude and high-speed bombers are two types which would give us a certain advantage again.

Referring to the small-scale attacks mounted by the *Höhenkampf Kommando* the previous year, Goering went on: 'For a high-altitude bomber I had to use the Ju 86, one of the oldest crates which were generally available for a few weeks to fill the gap. It carried a 50 kg [*sic*] bomb at certain altitudes.'[3]

In fact, Heinkel was already working on two high-altitude bomber projects. The first of these was a pressurised version of his dependable twin-engine medium bomber, the He 111. A single prototype was built, designated the He 111R-2, which was fitted with Daimler-Benz DB 603U engines with turbo-superchargers. The importance attached to the project can be gauged by the fact that in September 1942 the RLM placed it third by order of priority in a list of aircraft then under development by the company, behind only the He 177 heavy bomber and He 219 night-fighter. The He 111R-2 undertook test flights in early 1944 but failed to reach the anticipated altitude and so didn't enter production.

Heinkel's other high-altitude bomber was the He 274. The origins of this aircraft lay in the company's notoriously troublesome He 177 heavy bomber, a type for which the

Luftwaffe high command had great hopes, but which never fully overcame its serious reliability issues. These stemmed from its four coupled DB 601 engines, which were alarmingly prone to catching fire in flight (earning it the grim nickname 'The Flaming Coffin').

While the He 177 was under development, in April 1939 Heinkel proposed a high-altitude variant, the He 177H model (derived from the He 177 A4, optimised for high-altitude flight), which he hoped would be capable of flying at altitudes between 40–50,000ft. The RLM approved the proposal and two prototypes along with four pre-production aircraft were ordered in October 1941 for what had now been designated the He 274.

With Heinkel's German facilities operating at full capacity on existing projects, most of the design work for the He 274 and the construction of the prototypes was delegated to the French aircraft manufacturer SAUF (Societe Anonyme des Usines Farman), at its factory in Suresnes, Paris. Originally the Avions Farman, the company had been founded in 1908 and, with a background in heavy bombers and experimental high-altitude aircraft (having built the Farman F.1001, which made an attempt on the world altitude record in 1936), was a natural choice to assist Heinkel on the He 274.

The design of the new bomber diverged substantially from the He 177. Wisely, the coupled engine configuration was ditched in favour of a conventional layout of four separate DB 603A powerplants, the wing – of 145ft span – was redesigned, and rather than the He 177's single tailfin the designers settled on a twin tail unit. It was expected to be capable of carrying

8,800lbs of bombs, have a range of 2,140 miles and reach a maximum height of 47,000ft.

Work at the Suresnes factory on the first prototypes proceeded at a rather leisurely pace, the French workforce doing only the minimum required to avoid deportation to factories in Germany.

Based on intelligence passed on by the French Resistance, who had a source inside the Farman factory, the Allies were able to build up a fairly comprehensive picture of the new Heinkel bomber and progress of its development at Suresnes, as revealed in an Allied Intelligence report dated December 1943:

> The prototype is at the moment under construction at the Farman factory at Suresnes. Two fuselages have been constructed side-by-side. One will serve for static tests very shortly. The other, for actual flying, is now receiving its fittings to be despatched in about two months' time, to Rostock, where the engines and armament will be fitted and the flying trials commenced.[4]

Five months later another intelligence report was compiled on what the Allies were now calling the Farman He 274 stratospheric aircraft: 'This aircraft will have a weight of 77,500lb and a loading of 11lb per hp. It will be fitted with two superchargers, one of which is a new turbo-blower sent specially from Germany and having a special interest.'[5]

Consideration may have been given to sabotaging the factory and the prototypes, as the intelligence report also outlined details of the security arrangements at the Suresnes facility.

If there were any such plans, they were overtaken by events. As the first prototype, He 274 V1, was nearing completion in August 1944, the German personnel were forced to evacuate the factory as the advancing Allied armies approached Paris. Before leaving, an attempt had been made by the departing Germans to destroy the prototype with explosive charges fixed to the engines, but only minor damage was caused. Many of the original drawings and documents pertaining to the He 274 also survived.

From interviews with the French workers, Allied investigators discovered that Heinkel planned to build a limited series of twenty to forty He 274s, although the Germans' lack of trust in their French colleagues was evident from the fact that the local workforce was kept in the dark about certain aspects of the aircraft. 'They had very little exact knowledge of the aircraft characteristics or performance as the Germans only told them as little as possible about it,' Air Intelligence reported.

A later report from November 1944 also found that 'considerable trouble had been met with the pressure cabin, the first version leaking badly, particularly at rivet holes. The second version, as now fitted, was better, but the leaks had not been fully cured.'[6] The investigators who examined the prototype also noted that visibility through the heavily framed and double-glazed Plexiglas panels in the pressurised cockpit was poor.

After the war the He 274 V1 prototype was repaired and completed by the newly established French aviation firm AAS (Ateliers Aéronautiques de Suresnes). Renamed the 01A, it was used to aid high–altitude research work for the Armée de l'Air. The second prototype was also completed by AAS and joined the test programme in December 1947. Among the experiments carried out by the French with the two ex-He 274s were 'piggyback' flights, using the two bombers to carry aloft a jet aircraft fixed atop the fuselage and launch it in mid-flight, similar to those planned by the Germans using a Do 217K and the DFS 228 super high-altitude reconnaissance aircraft.

Both test aircraft were scrapped in 1953.

Rival projects

Besides Heinkel, several of Germany's other major aircraft manufacturers also tried to meet the Luftwaffe's need for a very high-altitude bomber. One of the He 274's main competitors was the Henschel Hs 130. This project had its roots in an experimental aircraft commissioned by the RLM in 1937, the Hs 128, for high-altitude research work. For this purpose, the Hs 128 was designed to incorporate a pressure cabin designed by the DVL, bolted into the nose section, and was fitted with a pair of DB 601 engines with a TK 9 turbo-supercharger.

The Hs 128 made its first flight on 11 April 1939 before being sent to Rechlin for an intensive programme of test flights. Though it couldn't reach the expected very high altitudes, the RLM was sufficiently impressed to order Henschel to develop the Hs 128 into an operational type. Designated the Hs 130, the RLM wanted two versions, one for reconnaissance (the Hs 130A) and one for bombing (the Hs 130B), and ordered six prototypes in 1939. The Hs 130 had a wingspan of just over 95ft and a pressure cabin that could be easily removed to be replaced by a new one, in the event of it being damaged in combat.

Work proceeded apace and by spring 1940 the first prototype was ready for testing, making its maiden flight on 23 May. A second prototype was completed in October. At this time priority was being given to the reconnaissance version, following a positive assessment of the aircraft by Oberst Theodor Rowehl, who test flew the prototype on 29 June 1940.[7] Therefore, the Hs 130B bomber was cancelled before any prototypes had been built. This decision notwithstanding, a revised bomber version, to be powered by BMW 801J engines and capable of carrying a 4,400lb bombload, designated the Hs 130C, was approved shortly thereafter. Other than featuring gun turrets above and below the pressure cabin, it differed little from the 'A' model. Production began in 1941, with ten examples being completed out of an initial order for thirty.

In September that year work began on an improved version. The Hs 130E had an extended wingspan, now measuring 108ft, and replaced the BMW powerplants with DB 603 units. The biggest change, however, was that it now carried a third engine (a DB 605T) in the lengthened fuselage, driving a two-stage supercharger to provide compressed air to the DB 603s, in an arrangement known as *Höhen-Zentrale*, or 'HZ'. The ten 'C' models already built were subsequently scrapped.

Flight testing of the Hs 130E prototype commenced in August 1942. A negative aspect of the design was that the crew access hatch was built into the roof of the cabin, making escape in an emergency for the crew a tricky business. This fact was highlighted on a test flight in December 1942, when the port engine caught fire after the Hs 130E reached 41,000ft. Soon the entire wing was ablaze, but of the three-man crew only the pilot succeeded in baling out through the hatch before the aircraft crashed. This prompted the addition of an emergency escape hatch in the floor of the cabin on future pre-production examples. Despite this, a second fatal crash struck the test programme on 24 September 1943, when the third Hs 130E prototype was lost on a test flight in Brandenburg, killing all crew members. Again, the cause was an engine fire.

These crashes caused the RLM to lose confidence in the Hs 130 programme. Henschel's problems, however, presented an opportunity for Dornier, which had been working on two related high-altitude bomber projects. The Do 317 was the company's submission for the 'Bomber B' competition, a requirement issued by the RLM in July 1939 to find a successor to the He 111, Do 17 and Ju 88 as the Luftwaffe's future standard medium bomber type.

The Do 317 was essentially a revised, enlarged version of the 217, equipped with a pressure cabin for its four-man crew and featuring unusual triangular tail fins. The 'Bomber B' competition was eventually won by Junkers' rival Ju 288,[8] but many of the Do 317's features were incorporated into the bomber version of the Do 217P reconnaissance aircraft, work on which had begun in late 1940 at the company's Friedrichshafen facility. Like the Hs 130E, the Do 217P would be powered by a combination of two DB 603 engines and a single DB 605T mounted in the fuselage to drive the supercharger. Three aircraft for development work were ordered.

Between 6 June and 22 October 1942 thirty-three test flights were carried out using the Do 217P V1 prototype (serial BK+IR). The first few flights went reasonably smoothly, with only a few minor faults being revealed. But the tenth flight, on 17 July, almost ended in disaster due to an engine fire. Fortunately, the crew managed to land the aircraft safely and the fire was put out. The 'HZ' system was also proving quite troublesome, though the technical issues associated with the set-up were eventually overcome. The greatest altitude achieved during this series of test flights was on 18 September, when a height of 42,650ft was reached. The following March an altitude of 44,700ft was attained.

The Do 217P's relatively trouble-free development contrasted sharply with that of the Hs 130. In April 1943 the RLM's Technical Office evaluated the two aircraft and reported on the state of development of the rival projects:

> At Henschel, flight testing the prototype and its equipment (defensive armament and release gear) will take until the end of the year, practically. On this basis, development aircraft (V series) cannot be expected before the beginning of 1944, and production aircraft not before spring/summer 1944. The Hs 130E represents a completely new expense in terms of money needed to complete the project.

> The prototype Do 217P complete with a supercharger intercooler could be produced in two to three months. A further five aircraft could be produced shortly thereafter. Producing an increased number of aircraft would involve little expense ... In contrast with the Hs 130E it is anticipated that there will not be any problems with constructing the fuselage, because all

of the relevant parts and components have been tested

. . Equipped with the new supercharger intercooler, the Do 217P attained speeds of between 600 and 650 km/h, at an altitude of 13,000 m, and demonstrated a maximum operating ceiling of 15,000 m.[9]

From this it can be seen that the RLM's clear preference was for the Do 217P, and six development aircraft were duly ordered. Nevertheless, with the Hs 130 having some influential backers, not least Rowehl, it was decided that work should also continue on that project. An initial production order for 100 aircraft was placed with Henschel, although continuing reliability problems with the engines and 'HZ' system would see this cut back to just thirty.

The Do 217P V1 and the third Hs 130E prototype were sent to Daimler-Benz's factory in Echterdingen near Stuttgart for further testing. With Daimler-Benz test pilot Flugkapitan Ellenrieder at the controls, the Hs 130E reached a height of 49,000ft on one occasion.[10] Two more Do 217P prototypes (V2 and V3) were completed by April 1943, but both were damaged in an Allied air raid on Dornier's Friedrichshafen works soon after, leaving the original prototype to continue as the sole test machine until repairs could be completed. The repaired V2 prototype was eventually written off after crashing on a test flight in March 1944. In April 1944 modifications were carried out to the airframe of the original Do 217P prototype at Friedrichshafen, including extending the wings, and passed on to the *Versuchsstelle für Höhenflüge* at Oranienburg, whose pilots managed to take it up to 49,800ft.

While the many technical issues associated with the two aircraft were slowly being conquered, neither the Do 217P nor the Hs 130E were destined to become operational. In an effort to rationalise the increasingly unmanageable number of aviation projects currently under development, and with the need for fighters for home defence by now the overriding priority, in February 1944 Milch decided to cancel the Hs 130. Two months later the axe also fell on the Do 217P.

Despite this, some limited testing work on both the Do 217P and Hs 130E development aircraft did continue, concerned with high-altitude flight research. All work on both projects ended definitively after the two remaining Dornier test aircraft, along with an Hs 130E and 130A model, were destroyed in an Allied air raid on the Daimler-Benz factory at Stuttgart on 5 September 1944.

RAF Air Intelligence learned more about the Hs 130 from Otto Oeckl, a Henschel engineer who fell into British hands after the German surrender. The intelligence report, based on information provided by Oeckl, stated that the Hs 130 was 'built to study the problems of high-altitude flying', but that the test aircraft 'were definitely underpowered for their purpose'. The report went on to state that: 'Although none of the projected sub-types of the Hs 130 ever became operational, this high-altitude aircraft aroused considerable interest when it was first identified.' It also revealed that, according to captured German documents, the Hs 130E model had a maximum range of 1,400 miles with a 2,200lb bombload and a ceiling of 47,500ft.[11]

Junkers enters the fray

Junkers, naturally, also became involved in the race to meet Hitler's demand for a new extreme altitude heavy bomber. Their initial plan was to develop the Ju 86R into a much larger aircraft with an even longer wingspan, the Ju 286, which would be powered by no fewer than six Jumo 208 engines. But this ambitious design never advanced beyond the drawing board.

Junkers' efforts then increasingly focused on its Ju 388, which grew out of both the Ju 188 and the ill-fated Ju 288. As previously noted, three versions of the Ju 388 were put into development, all intended for high-altitude operations: the 'L' (reconnaissance); the 'J' (night-fighter/*zerstörer*); and the 'K' (bomber) model. The bomber variant would have a range of 1,100 miles and could carry a maximum bombload of 6,600lbs, while defensive armament consisted of two MG 131 machine-guns in the tail turret. The maximum ceiling was 43,000ft.

The Ju 388K prototype was completed in January 1944 and made its maiden flight on 2 April, with the first of a batch of ten pre-production models rolling off the assembly line at Junkers' Merseburg factory in July. In December 1943 the RLM's Technical Office had laid down ambitious plans for the production of 900 bombers per month, 135 of these to be Ju 388Ks, with construction dispersed to thirteen separate sites. This plan, of course, was completely unrealistic, taking no account of Germany's dwindling resources and the impact Allied bombing was having on industrial output. In fact, little more than 100 Ju 388s were produced by war's end, of which only a handful were the 'K' version. The Ju 388K was cancelled in September 1944, following a decision reached by the Nazi high command in the summer to downgrade priority of bombers and other types in favour of fighters for home defence.

Junkers final attempt to produce a very high-altitude heavy bomber was the Ju 488, which was first proposed in December 1943. To speed up production, it was composed of parts from the Ju 188E (the rear fuselage) and the Ju 388K (the pressurised cabin), while the tail unit came from the abandoned Ju 288. The Ju 488 would have a lengthened fuselage and extended wings, carrying four BMW 802 engines, giving it a maximum speed of 367 mph and a range of 3,000 miles. The bombload was to be the same as the Ju 388K, at 6,600lbs, and it would have a ceiling of 42,000ft. A post-war Allied intelligence report on the bomber also mentions that it was intended to be equipped with an ejection seat.

With Junkers' German facilities all at full capacity, as in the case of Heinkel's He 274 development work on the new bomber was farmed out to a French aviation firm, in this case Breguet, at its factory in Montaudran near Toulouse. Ten pre-production aircraft were ordered. But as the first example (code number V.401) was nearing completion, on the night of 16/17 July 1944 a group of French Resistance fighters launched an audacious attack on the Breguet factory, destroying V.401 with hand grenades. A second Ju 488 that had been under construction at the factory was later found abandoned by a railway track nearby, as it was being transported back to Germany. The liberation of southern France and capture of the Breguet factory by US forces the following month brought all work on the Ju 488 project to an end.

Beyond the stratosphere

Although not strictly falling within the bounds of this work – being a proposal for a rocket-powered rather than piston-engined aircraft – the most extraordinary high-altitude bomber project conceived by the Germans during the war deserves a mention.

The Sänger Silbervogel ('Silverbird') was a truly fantastical concept, straight out of the realms of science-fiction. Dreamed up in the late 1930s by the Austrian scientist and rocketry expert Eugen Sänger, the Silbervogel was more spacecraft than military bomber, intended to fly at the upper reaches of the stratosphere and beyond. An extremely sleek, clean design, it was to be powered by two rocket motors in the rear of the slim fuselage, with the pilot housed in what Sänger described as an 'airtight stratosphere chamber' in the nose.

It would be launched at supersonic speed into the air from a rocket-powered sled fixed on a set of rails almost two miles long. Once airborne its own rocket motors would take it up to the incredible height of 490,000ft, putting the craft firmly into the mesosphere. The Silbervogel would then glide down and bounce off the denser air in the stratosphere, causing it to gain altitude again. Sänger likened this to the effect of a flat stone skimming across the surface of water.[12]

Flying at hypersonic speed, the Silbervogel would be capable of attacking targets many thousands of miles away with its 8,800lb bombload. Sänger suggested that a force of some 100 of these rocket bombers could completely obliterate any large city in a matter of days.

He produced a highly detailed proposal for his rocket bomber concept, some 900 pages long, but the technology of the time was not sufficiently advanced to turn Sänger's hugely ambitious vision into reality, and unsurprisingly the Silbervogel project was rejected out of hand when presented to the RLM in December 1941.

Assessing the threat

Fears that the Germans might resume their high-altitude bombing campaign against Britain, perhaps with a new generation of pressurised heavy bombers, led Field Marshal Sir Alan Brooke, Chief of the Imperial General Staff, to instruct a Joint Intelligence Sub-Committee to examine the threat. The Sub-Committee's report, which assessed and forecast 'the possibility and probable scale of enemy attack on the United Kingdom by high-altitude bombers operating up to 43,000ft, during 1943, 1944 and 1945', was delivered on 29 April 1943.[13]

The report opened by outlining the capabilities and threat posed by the only known high-altitude bomber currently in service with the Luftwaffe, the Junkers Ju 86R, of which the report's authors were unimpressed, in spite of the great difficulties Fighter Command had experienced in shooting any down over England the previous year. Dismissing it as 'an obsolescent type', which is 'not in itself a practical high-altitude bomber', the Sub-Committee judged that due to its rather paltry bombload the threat from this aircraft was negligible, even if the Germans were to deploy the Ju 86R in greater numbers: 'Increased production of this type would not of itself mean any great offensive threat to the United Kingdom in view of its limited bomb load.'[14]

The Sub-Committee was obviously ignorant of the multiple high-altitude bomber projects which were at that time under development in Germany, for their report continued:

> There is no evidence of any new type of German bomber being developed specifically for high altitude operations, and it is unlikely that, during 1943 or 1944, any new types will be produced with a greatly increased effective operational bombing ceiling above that of the present standard of German bombers. 1945 is rather too remote to enable a precise forecast of possibilities to be made.

However, the report was accurate in judging that 'demands on the German aircraft industry for current requirements are likely to be so heavy as to preclude the bringing into operation, even in 1945, of bombers of a high altitude type on any large scale'.[15]

The Sub-Committee anticipated that during 1944 the maximum operational ceiling of the standard bombers then in service with the Luftwaffe would probably increase, though this would be 'dependent upon the success of several technical developments, such as the production of new types of engine, the fitting of exhaust driven super-chargers and the development and production of sealed pressure cabins'. Even with technical advances in these areas, the British thought it 'very unlikely that a ceiling above 37,000ft will be reached'.[16]

One reason for the Sub-Committee's scepticism regarding the Nazis' ability to field a new generation of pressurised bombers in numbers in the near future were the physical problems associated with sustained high-altitude flight on aircrews, as their report explained:

> Apart from the difficulties of technical developments which would tend to retard the production of new types of high altitude bombers in quantity or the modification of existing bombers for that purpose, there is the human element to be considered, which is also bound to restrict the rapid development of high flying technique. The training of crews and their protection from the effects of damage to sealed pressure cabins by gunfire and experimentation of what would happen to crews which had to bale out at sub-stratospheric heights, all present problems which the enemy have not yet tackled on a large scale and would inevitably retard the date when this high altitude form of bombing could assume large operational proportions.[17]

In fact, unknown to the Allies at this time, the Germans had investigated these problems. Since 1942 German scientists, led by Dr Sigmund Rascher of the SS, had been conducting a programme of research into the physical effects of extreme altitude flight on the human body, using concentration camp inmates as human guinea pigs. The full details of these chilling experiments only came to light at the Nuremberg war crimes trials after the war.

In an affidavit to the court dated 1 November 1946, Dr Hans Romberg, a scientist at the DVL who assisted Rascher in his macabre work, confirmed that 'from about March 1942 to about the end of May 1942 experiments were conducted at the Dachau concentration camp to determine the effects of extreme high altitudes on the human body. These experiments were conducted for the benefit of the Luftwaffe.'

Dr Romberg went on to reveal that a portable low-pressure chamber was used for these experiments:

> This chamber could duplicate atmospheric conditions and pressures prevailing at high altitudes. It consisted of two parts, one of which was used for slow ascensions and descensions and could accommodate as many as twelve people at a time, while the other was used for explosive decompression and could accommodate only one or two people.
> [...]
> When prisoners were requested, we asked that they be in a physical condition which compared with members of the Luftwaffe.

Romberg also revealed the human cost of these experiments, stating that he personally 'witnessed the death of three of Dr Rascher's human experimental subjects during the experiments. I know that other experimental subjects were killed while I was not present and I would estimate that they totalled between five and ten.'

In a captured report written by Dr Rascher, dated 11 May 1942, he stated that the results of his experiments confirmed that baling out of an aircraft at an altitude of 42,000ft and above was practically impossible, 'since at that height the bends appear rather suddenly'. He suggested that ejection seats offered the only realistic means for the crew to successfully escape at such heights and that they would have to be equipped with breathing apparatus because 'descending with opened parachute without oxygen would cause severe injuries due to the lack of oxygen, besides causing severe freezing; consciousness would not be regained until the ground was reached'.[18]

The Joint Intelligence Sub-Committee's report concluded by assuring the War Cabinet that 'the scale of attack from high-altitude bombers during 1943 is likely to be sufficiently small to justify its being ignored'. Due to the numerous technical challenges involved, they also assessed that by 1944 the number of enemy pressurised bombers capable of operating at extreme altitude:

> is likely to be small, by which is meant a scale of effort produced by a total force of up to, say, thirty high altitude aircraft, resulting in spasmodic attacks by single or possibly two or three aircraft at a time. We believe that the same would hold good for 1945, although obviously a forecast for so distant a time must be more conjectural.[19]

In the event, despite intensive efforts, German industry failed to produce the high-altitude *vergeltung* bombers Hitler craved to strike back at Britain, and there would be no repeat of the stratospheric Ju 86R mini-raids of August – September 1942.

Conclusion

As can be seen in the preceding chapters, the vast majority of extreme altitude aircraft developed by both the Allied and Axis powers during the Second World War did not enter operational service. Many did not progress beyond the prototype stage; others remained 'paper projects' only. There were various reasons for this: shifting priorities as the strategic situation facing the belligerents changed with the fortunes of war or, in the case of Germany and Japan, lack of resources, disruption to industry caused by enemy bombing and, ultimately, time simply running out.

But some of those aircraft which did make it to the frontline squadrons played a highly significant role in influencing the course of events at various points in the war. The Junkers Ju 86P and the later, improved, R model provided the Luftwaffe with an extremely valuable – if mechanically temperamental – PR platform, which in the first half of the war was the one German type capable of penetrating enemy airspace with near impunity. The failure to introduce an effective successor in the high-altitude PR role left the Luftwaffe with a critical gap in its capabilities, one that wouldn't be filled until the arrival of the revolutionary Arado Ar 234 jet in August 1944 – too late to make any difference in a war that had by then turned decisively against the Nazis.

A similar situation prevailed in the Pacific. Until 1943 the JAAF's excellent Mitsubishi Ki-46 reconnaissance aircraft, able to fly higher than anything else stationed in the Far East, roamed the skies with little chance of interception, until improved fighter opposition finally brought its era of supremacy to an end.

The Allies also looked to high-flying aircraft to bring their precious reconnaissance photographs back safely. The legendary Spitfire proved well-suited to the PR role, and in its ultimate PR.Mk XIX guise was capable of reaching 44,000ft, making it a very difficult target, even when the Luftwaffe began receiving Me 262 jet interceptors. So good were the PR versions of the Spitfire that they became one of the very few aircraft of foreign origin to be adopted by the USAAF during the war.

As for bombers, despite a plethora of projects being instigated by the US, Britain, Germany and Japan, only three pressurised bombers that could attack from great altitudes saw active service – the Junkers Ju 86R, the de Havilland Mosquito B.Mk XVI, and the Boeing B-29 Superfortress. The Luftwaffe's high-altitude raids on southern England in 1942 – using just four Ju 86R reconnaissance aircraft modified for the task – were mere pinpricks, which achieved little beyond some fleeting domestic propaganda gains. The Mosquito B.Mk XVI used by the RAF against Germany was a greater threat, with its 4,000lb bombload, but generally carried out its raids below 30,000ft.

It was in the Pacific theatre where the pressurised bomber would have the greatest impact. American industrial might ensured that several thousand Boeing B-29 Superfortresses rolled off the production lines, allowing the USAAF to conduct a massive, sustained bombing campaign against Japan from bases 1,500 miles away. Although the initial results of this campaign were disappointing, with the lack of bombing accuracy at high altitude prompting a switch to low-to-medium altitude bombing at night, the B-29 unquestionably was the single most important factor in Japan's defeat.

Fears sparked by these aircraft, and others under development by the major warring nations, spurred development of a large array of pressurised interceptor projects to combat the threat they posed. For the British and the Germans, the threat either failed to materialise or amounted to only a few very small-scale raids, so that those high-altitude fighters that did enter operational service rarely got the opportunity to perform in their intended role.

The Japanese, of course, had the most pressing need for such aircraft. But despite intensive efforts in the latter part of the war, Japanese industry – hobbled by shortages of vital resources, a lack of technical expertise regarding the production of the necessary turbo-superchargers, and the B-29 raids themselves – was unable to provide the JAAF and JNAF with the fighters they so desperately required to defeat the Superfortress. Many of these same problems also frustrated their dreams of striking back at America with their own pressurised super bombers.

The race to reach ever higher into the stratosphere did not, of course, end in 1945. During the Cold War, the US and Britain would continue to develop aircraft that depended on great height to avoid the enemy's air defences. Within a few years of the end of the Second World War, a new generation of jet-powered spy planes like the English Electric Canberra and

Lockheed U-2 would be routinely conducting reconnaissance missions at altitudes of 60,000ft and more. These, in turn, would be eclipsed by Lockheed's awesome SR-71 'Blackbird' and the Soviet MiG-25 'Foxbat' interceptor/reconnaissance aircraft. Capable of reaching over 85,000 and 120,000ft, respectively, these aircraft were the ultimate manned high-flyers, soaring into the stratosphere at heights the designers and airmen who pushed back the boundaries of high-altitude flight during the Second World War could only dream of.[1]

Details of main high-altitude aircraft types of Second World War

Arado Ar 240

User:	Luftwaffe
Type:	Reconnaissance
Introduced:	1943
Crew:	2
Powerplant:	2 x Daimler-Benz DB 601A
Maximum speed:	410 mph
Service ceiling:	34,450ft

Boeing B-29, F-13

User:	USAAF
Type:	Bomber/Reconnaissance
Introduced:	1944
Crew:	10 – 13
Powerplant:	4 x Wright Duplex Cyclone R-3350
Maximum speed:	357 mph
Service ceiling:	33,600ft

de Havilland Mosquito Mk XV

User:	RAF
Type:	Fighter/Night-fighter
Introduced:	1942
Crew:	2
Powerplant:	2 x Rolls-Royce Merlin 61
Maximum speed:	408 mph
Service ceiling:	43,800ft

de Havilland Mosquito B.Mk XVI, PR.Mk XVI

User:	RAF, USAAF (PR.MK XVI)
Type:	Bomber/Reconnaissance
Introduced:	1944
Crew:	2
Powerplant:	2 x Rolls-Royce Merlin 72 V-12
Maximum speed:	416 mph
Service ceiling:	42,000ft

de Havilland Mosquito PR.Mk 34

User:	RAF
Type:	Reconnaissance
Introduced:	1944
Crew:	2
Powerplant:	2 x Rolls-Royce Merlin 113/114
Maximum speed:	422 mph
Service ceiling:	43,000ft

Focke-Wulf Ta 152H

User:	Luftwaffe
Type:	Fighter
Introduced:	1945
Crew:	1
Powerplant:	1 x Jumo 213E-1
Maximum speed:	469 mph
Service ceiling:	49,540ft

Junkers Ju 86P-2

User:	Luftwaffe
Type:	Reconnaissance
Introduced:	1940
Crew:	2
Powerplant:	2 x Jumo 207A-1
Maximum speed:	248 mph
Service ceiling:	42,000ft

Junkers Ju 86R-1, R-2

User:	Luftwaffe
Type:	Reconnaissance (R-1)/Bomber (R-2)
Introduced:	1942
Crew:	2
Powerplant:	2 x Jumo 207B-3
Maximum speed:	260 mph
Service ceiling:	45,900ft

Junkers Ju 388L

User:	Luftwaffe
Type:	Reconnaissance
Introduced:	1945
Crew:	3
Powerplant:	2 x BMW 801TJ
Maximum speed:	383 mph
Service ceiling:	43,000ft

*Messerschmitt Bf 109G-1, -3, -5***

User:	Luftwaffe
Type:	Fighter
Introduced:	1943
Crew:	1
Powerplant:	Daimler-Benz DB 605
Maximum speed:	426 mph
Service ceiling:	41,400ft

Messerschmitt Bf 109H

User:	Luftwaffe
Type:	Reconnaissance
Introduced:	1944
Crew:	1
Powerplant:	1 x Daimler-Benz DB 628
Maximum speed:	427 mph
Service ceiling:	47,500ft

Messerschmitt Bf 109K-4

User:	Luftwaffe
Type:	Fighter
Introduced:	1944
Crew:	1
Powerplant:	1 x Daimler-Benz DB 605DM
Maximum speed:	452 mph
Service ceiling:	41,000ft

Supermarine Spitfire Mk VI

User:	RAF
Type:	Fighter
Introduced:	1942
Crew:	1
Powerplant:	1 x Rolls-Royce Merlin 47
Maximum speed:	356 mph
Service ceiling:	39,200ft

Supermarine Spitfire Mk VII

User:	RAF
Type:	Fighter
Introduced:	1943
Crew:	1
Powerplant:	1 x Rolls-Royce Merlin 64, 71
Maximum speed:	408 mph
Service ceiling:	44,000ft

Supermarine Spitfire PR.Mk X

User:	RAF
Type:	Reconnaissance
Introduced:	1944
Crew:	1
Powerplant:	1 x Rolls-Royce Merlin 77
Maximum speed:	416 mph
Service ceiling:	40,000ft

Supermarine Spitfire PR.Mk XIX

User:	RAF, USAAF
Type:	Reconnaissance
Introduced:	1944
Crew:	1
Powerplant:	1 x Rolls-Royce Griffon 65
Maximum speed:	442 mph
Service ceiling:	44,000ft

* Aircraft with pressurised cabins which entered operational service during the Second World War
** Details refer to Bf 109G-5 model

Appendix B

Junkers Ju 86R bombing raids on the United Kingdom

Date	Location	Comments
24/8/42	Camberley	Unknown casualties
24/8/42	Southampton	1 killed
25/8/42	Stanstead St Margarets	Unknown casualties
28/8/42	Bristol	47 killed, 50 injured
28/8/42	Cardiff	2 killed, several injured
29/8/42	Swindon	8 killed, 6 injured
29/8/42	Cambridge	Unknown casualties
30/8/42	Chelmsford	No casualties
4/9/42	Ramsgate	Unknown casualties
5/9/42	Luton	4 killed
6/9/42	Aldershot	Unknown casualties
9/9/42	Near Clacton	Unknown casualties
11/9/42	Poole	5 killed
12/9/42	Salisbury	No casualties. Ju 86R (T5+PM) damaged in combat with Spitfire BF273

Notes

Introduction

1. Due to differences in the air temperature, nearer the equator the stratosphere begins at around 56,000ft.
2. The Italian Giulio Douhet was the leading proponent of the theory that aerial bombing would be the decisive factor in future warfare.

Chapter One: The Quest for Altitude

1. The first German airship to be shot down over Britain was SL11, destroyed by Lieutenant William Leefe Robinson over Cuffley in Hertfordshire on the night of 3 September 1916. The feat earned Leefe Robinson the Victoria Cross.
2. *Military History Magazine*, March 1997 issue.
3. von Lünen, *Under the Waves, Above the Clouds: A History of the Pressure Suit*, p.165–166.
4. www.history.nasa.gov
5. Wiley Post was killed along with his passenger Will Rogers when his aircraft crashed in a lagoon during a long-range flight on 15 August 1935.
6. *Sydney Morning Herald*, 1 October 1936.
7. *Air Forces* magazine, Vol. 82, No. 7, July 1999. As the Soviet Union was not a member of the *Fédération Aéronautique Internationale*, the body that verifies flight records, Kokkinaki's world altitude record claim was not officially recognised.
8. The service ceiling is the altitude at which an aircraft can climb no higher than 100ft per minute. The absolute ceiling is the altitude at which an aircraft can climb no higher.

9. Chambers, *Junkers Military Aircraft of World War Two*, p.54–55
10. www.spacemedicineassociation.org
11. The first enemy aircraft to be shot down over the British Isles in the Second World War was a Heinkel He 111 of KG 26, which fell to Spitfires of No 602 and 603 Squadron while on a PR sortie to photograph shipping at the Rosyth naval base on 28 October 1939, crashing in the village of Humbie near Edinburgh.
12. www.spacemedicineassociation.org

Chapter Two: The Junkers Ju 86P

1. Chambers, *Junkers Military Aircraft of World War Two*, p.12.
2. Neuenhofen was killed in January 1936 while test flying a Ju 87 'Stuka'.
3. Chambers, op. cit., p.48.
4. Ibid. p.51.
5. Ibid. p.52.
6. Dressel; Griehl, *Junkers Ju 86*, p.44.
7. Sommer, *Luftwaffe Eagle*, p.87.
8. *Fight Above the Clouds*, Eureka Media Inc, 2013.

Chapter Three: *Kommando* Rowehl

1. Bowyer, *Air War Over Europe*, p.156.
2. Kahn, *Hitler's Spies*, p.113.
3. Nuremberg Trial proceedings, 18 March 1946. The ambitious Anglo-French plan to cripple the Soviet Union's oil production in the Caucasus, codenamed Operation Pike, was repeatedly postponed before eventually being abandoned in May 1940 after Hitler launched his assault on France.
4. Price, *Spitfire: A Documentary History*, p.101.
5. National Archives, Kew: CAB 80/28/1
6. National Archives, Kew: AIR 40/182
7. Ibid.
8. Ibid.
9. Kahn, op. cit., p.114.

10. Ketley; Thomas, *Luftwaffe KG 200: The German Air Force's Most Secret Unit of World War II*, p.43.

Chapter Four: Flying from Kastelli

1. National Archives, Kew: AIR 27/9/6.
2. Ibid.
3. Ibid.
4. In official documents, both DAF pilots and the Air Intelligence Branch tended to erroneously refer to the type as the Ju 86P, rather than the Ju 86R.
5. National Archives, Kew: AIR 40/182.
6. Kent, *One of the Few*, p.199 (Extracts reproduced with permission of the Licensor through PLS Clear).
7. Cull, *Fighters Over the Aegean*, p.182, 183.
8. *London Gazette*, 7 April 1942.
9. National Archives, Kew: AIR 27/985/33.
10. National Archives, Kew: AIR 27/2070/11.
11. Op. cit., AIR 27/985/33.
12. Cull, op. cit., p.186.
13. National Archives, Kew: AIR 50/448/4.
14. Cull, op. cit., p.188–189.
15. National Archives, Kew: AIR 40/182.
16. Ibid.
17. National Archives, Kew: AIR 27/670/35.
18. National Archives, Kew: AIR 27/917/21.
19. Kent, op. cit., p.199-200.
20. Price, *The Spitfire Story*, p.168.
21. Isby, *The Decisive – Spitfire vs 109*, p.270, 271.
22. National Archives, Kew: AIR 27/670/37.
23. Ibid.
24. National Archives, Kew: AIR 27/917/23.
25. Cull, op. cit., p.195.
26. Ibid. p.240.

Chapter Five: Strato Spits

1. Isby, *The Decisive Duel – Spitfire vs 109*, p.144
2. Grehan; Mace (editors), *Defending Britain's Skies 1940 – 1945*, p.40
3. Clostermann, *The Big Show: Some Experiences of a French Fighter Pilot in the RAF*, p.99.
4. Price, *The Spitfire Story*, p.147
5. Ibid. p.150–151.
6. Ibid. p.150.
7. Dibbs; Holmes, *Spitfire: Flying Legend*, p.51–52 (Extracts reproduced with permission of the Licensor through PLS Clear).
8. National Archives, Kew: AIR 27/2126/53.
9. National Archives, Kew: AIR 27/2126/55.
10. National Archives, Kew: AIR 27/2126/57.
11. National Archives, Kew: AIR 27/919/27.
12. National Archives, Kew: AIR 27/2126/61.
13. National Archives, Kew: AIR 27/2126/83.
14. National Archives, Kew: AIR 27/2076/21.
15. National Archives, Kew: AIR 27/934/33.
16. Price, op. cit., p.177.
17. Price, *Spitfire: Pilots' Stories*, p.148 (Extract reproduced with permission of the Licensor through PLS Clear).
18. Dibbs; Holmes, op. cit., p.130–131.
19. National Archives, Kew: AIR 27/919/39.
20. National Archives, Kew: AIR 50/47/16.
21. National Archives, Kew: AIR 27/2126/83.
22. Dibbs; Holmes, op. cit., p.130–131.
23. Downing, *Spies in the Sky*, p.36.
24. National Archives, Kew: AIR 27/2013/29.
25. Ibid.
26. National Archives, Kew: AIR 27/2013/27.
27. Price, *Dogfight: True Stories of Dramatic Air Actions*, p.88.
28. On 5 February 1952, a Spitfire PR.XIX of No 81 Squadron, based at Kai Tak in Hong Kong and flown by Flt Lt Ted Powles, reached

a phenomenal height of 50,000ft (indicated) during a meteorological sortie to record air temperatures at high altitude in the area. This is believed to be greatest altitude achieved by a Spitfire.

29. National Archives, Kew: AIR 27/2013/49.
30. Isby, op. cit., p.273.
31. Dibbs; Holmes, op. cit., p.121.

Chapter Six: Replacing the Ju 86R

1. Suprun was killed in action on 4 July 1941 while flying a MiG-3.
2. National Archives, Kew: HW 1/2078.
3. Sommer, *Luftwaffe Eagle*, p.203.
4. National Archives, Kew: AIR 27/1728/27.
5. National Archives, Kew: HW 1/2078.
6. Forsyth, *Junkers Ju 188 Units of WW2*, p.54.
7. US Air Materiel Command, Junkers Ju 388L technical report (October 1946).
8. National Archives, Kew: AIR 27/919/45.
9. National Archives, Kew: AIR 27/919/48.
10. National Archives, Kew: AIR 27/919/50.
11. National Archives, Kew: AIR 27/2078/3.
12. National Archives, Kew: CAB 79/74/2.
13. Peter Ayerst interview, IWM sound archive.
14. Kahn, *Hitler's Spies*, p.128.
15. Darlow, *Victory Fighters: The Veterans' Story*, p.91.
16. www.ghostbombers.com.
17. Ibid.
18. Price, *Dogfight – True Stories of Dramatic Air Actions*, p.264.

Chapter Seven: Fighters in the Heavens

1. National Archives, Kew: CAB 80/28/1.
2. National Archives, Kew: CAB 79/11/26.
3. Grehan; Mace (editors), *Defending Britain's Skies 1940–45*, p.164.
4. Corduroy, *Whirlwind: Westland's Enigmatic Fighter*, p.49.

5. www.baesystems.com/en/heritage.
6. National Archives, Kew: AIR 2/5583.
7. Harald Penrose interview, IWM sound archive.
8. *London Gazette*, 27 July 1943.
9. Philip Gadesden Lucas interview, IWM sound archive.
10. *Fight Above the Clouds* documentary, (Eureka Media, 2013).
11. National Archvies, Kew: AIR 37/587.
12. National Archives, Kew: AIR 20/6044.
13. Ibid.
14. Op. cit., AIR 37/587.
15. Op. cit., AIR 20/6044.
16. Ibid.
17. Ibid.

Chapter Eight: Stratospheric *Störangriffe*

1. https://en.wikipedia.org.wiki/Area_bombing_directive
2. Goebbels, *The Goebbels Diaries, 1942–1943*, p.154.
3. Price, *Blitz on Britain*, p.150.
4. Sommer, *Luftwaffe Eagle*, p.90.
5. Ibid. p.90.
6. National Archives, Kew: AIR 40/182.
7. Ibid.
8. Ibid.
9. Ibid.
10. Sommer, op. cit., p.91.
11. National Archives, Kew: AIR 27/1548/14
12. *The Glasgow Herald*, 29 August 1942
13. *Bristol Post*, 23 August 2022.
14. Op. cit., AIR 40/182.
15. Ibid.
16. National Archives, Kew: CAB 65/27/35.
17. National Archives, Kew: AIR 27/919/31.
18. National Archives, Kew: AIR 27/1681/17.
19. National Archives, Kew: AIR 27/2126/61.

20. National Archives, Kew: CAB 195/1/36.
21. National Archives, Kew: AIR 2/5583.
22. Ibid.
23. Ibid.
24. www.peoplesmosquito.org.uk.
25. National Archives, Kew: AIR 27/2110/39.
26. Price, *Spitfire: A Documentary History*, p.104.
27. Price, *Blitz on Britain*, op. cit., p.157.
28. National Archives, Kew: AIR 27/1951/17.
29. National Archives, Kew: AIR 50/396.
30. Sommer, op. cit., p.93.
31. Op. cit., AIR 50/396.
32. Sommer, op. cit., p.98.
33. Ibid., p.99.
34. Op. cit., AIR 2/5583.
35. Ibid.
36. National Archives, Kew: AVIA 18/716.
37. www.peoplesmosquito.org.uk

Chapter Nine: Luftwaffe *Höhenjägers*

1. Anon., *The Strategic Air Offensive Against Germany: 1939–1945*, p.306.
2. Von Lünen, *Under the Waves, Above the Clouds: A History of the Pressure Suit*, p.130.
3. www.bbc.co.uk/history/ww2peopleswar
4. Francis Jones interview, IWM sound archive.
5. Holland, *Dam Busters – the Race to Smash the Dams*, p.87.
6. Brown, *Wings On My Sleeve*, p.88 (Extract reproduced with permission of the Licensor through PLS Clear).
7. Ibid. p.88.
8. Sharp, *Secret Projects of the Luftwaffe: Blohm & Voss BV 155*, p.9. The final major production variant of the 109 incorporating cockpit pressurisation was the Bf 109K-4, which entered service in October 1944.
9. Ibid. p.10.
10. Ibid. p.10.

11. Price, *Focke-Wulf Fw 190 in Combat*, p.8–9 (Extract reproduced with permission of the Licensor through PLS Clear).
12. Sharp, op. cit., p.64.
13. *Sternenbanner*, February 1944 issue.
14. Sharp, op. cit., p.81.
15. The captured BV 155 is currently in storage at the National Air and Space Museum in Washington, DC.
16. Price, op. cit., p.9.
17. National Archives, Kew: AIR 27/1934/72.
18. Sharp, *Spitfires Over Berlin*, p.92.
19. Op. cit., AIR 27/1934/72.
20. Sharp, *Spitfires Over Berlin*, op. cit., p.92.
21. Ibid., p.93.
22. MacIntyre, *Agent Zigzag*, p.84.
23. Graf reputedly reached an altitude of 46,885ft on one occasion in a Bf 109G-5 in 1943.
24. National Archives, Kew: AVIA 18/716.
25. National Archives, Kew: AIR 27/2044/15.
26. Iredale, *The Pathfinders*, pp. 332, 334.
27. Forsyth, *Junkers Ju 188 Units of WW2*, p.67.
28. www.airandspace.si.edu/collection-objects/ruhrstahl-x-4-missile/nasm

Chapter Ten: Japan versus the Superforts

1. Isby, *The Decisive Duel – Spitfire Vs. 109*, p.319.
2. National Archives, Kew: AIR 27/2124/1
3. The Allies gave male names to Japanese fighters, female ones to bombers, reconnaissance and transport aircraft.
4. The Consolidated B-32 'Dominator' was itself dogged with development problems and would only eventually enter service, in small numbers, in summer 1945.
5. www.andersen.af.mil
6. Sakaida; Takai, *B-29 Hunters of the JAAF*, p.9.
7. Gallagher, *Meatballs and Dead Birds*, p.102.

8. *United States Strategic Bombing Survey Report (Pacific War)*, p.16.
9. The DC4E was later reported by the Japanese to have crashed in Tokyo Bay. In fact, it had been passed on to Nakajima for study.
10. One of the G8N1 prototypes was destroyed on the ground in a strafing attack by US Navy fighters in June 1945.
11. Dyer, *Japanese Secret Projects – Experimental Aircraft of the IJA and IJN 1939 – 1945*, p.108.

Chapter Eleven: Hitler's Retaliation Bombers

1. Emme, Eugene M., *Hitler's Blitzbomber*, p.13.
2. Heinkel, *Stormy Life*, p.206.
3. Sharp, *Luftwaffe: Secret Bombers of the Third Reich*, p.69.
4. Ibid. p.47.
5. Ibid. p.47.
6. Ibid. p.49.
7. Griehl, *Do 217 – 317 – 417: An Operational Record*, p.177.
8. The Junkers Ju 288 would never enter service, being cancelled in 1943, largely due to development problems with the chosen Jumo 222 powerplant.
9. Griehl, op. cit., p.177–178.
10. Ibid., p.178.
11. Sharp, op. cit., p.25.
12. Ibid. p.95.
13. National Archives, Kew: CAB 79/60/47.
14. Ibid.
15. Ibid.
16. Ibid.
17. Ibid.
18. https://nuremberg.law.harvard.edu/documents/4093.
19. Op. cit., National Archives, CAB 79/60/47.

Conclusion

1. On 31 August 1977, a modified MiG 25 'Foxbat', flown by Soviet pilot Aleksandr Vasilyevich Fedotov, set an absolute world altitude record of 123,523ft – a record which stands to this day.

Bibliography

Bowyer, Chaz, *Air War Over Europe* (Pen & Sword, 2003)

Brown, Eric, *Wings On My Sleeve* (Weidenfeld & Nicholson, 2007)

Chambers, Mark A., *Junkers Military Aircraft of World War Two* (The History Press, 2017)

Clostermann, Pierre, *The Big Show* (Chatto and Windus, 1951)

Corduroy, Niall, *Whirlwind: Westland's Enigmatic Fighter* (Fonthill, 2017)

Cull, Brian, *Fighters Over the Aegean* (Fonthill Media, 2017)

Darlow, Stephen, *Victory Fighters: The Veterans' Story* (Bounty Books, 2007)

Davies, Glyn, *From Lysander to Lightning: Teddy Petter, Aircraft Designer* (The History Press, 2014)

Dibbs, John and Holmes, Tony, *Spitfire: Flying Legend* (Osprey, 1999)

Downing, Taylor, *Spies in the Sky* (Little Brown, 2011)

Dressel, Joachim and Griehl, Manfred, *Junkers Ju 86* (Schiffer, 1998)

Dyer, Edwin M., *Japanese Secret Projects – Experimental Aircraft of the IJA and IJN 1939-1945* (Midland, 2009)

Emme, Eugene M., *Hitler's Blitzbomber* (US Air University, 1951)

Forsyth, Robert, *Junkers Ju 188 Units of WW2* (Osprey, 2022)

Gallagher, James, *Meatballs and Dead Birds* (Stackpole, 2004)

Goebbels, Josef (ed. Louis P. Lochner), *The Goebbels Diaries Vol. – 1942 – 1943* (Doubleday, 1948)

Grehan, John and Mace, Martin, *Defending Britain's Skies 1940-45* (Pen & Sword, 2014)

Griehl, Manfred, *Do 217 – 317 – 417: An Operational Record* (Airlife, 1991)

Heinkel, Ernst, *Stormy Life* (E.P. Dutton, 1951)

Holland, James, *Dam Busters – The Race to Smash the Dams* (Corgi, 2013)

Iredale, Will, *The Pathfinders* (WH Allen, 2021)

Isby, David, *The Deadly Duel – Spitfire Vs 109* (Abacus, 2013)

Kahn, David, *Hitler's Spies* (Arrow, 1978)

Ketley, Barry and Thomas, Geoffrey J., *Luftwaffe KG 200: The German Air Force's Most Secret Unit of World War II* (Stackpole, 2015)

Mason, Tim, *The Secret Years: Flight Testing at Boscombe Down 1935 – 1945* (Crecy, 2010)

Moore, Jason Nicholas, *Soviet Fighters of the Second World War* (Fonthill, 2021)

Price, Alfred, *Blitz on Britain* (Sutton, 2000)

_____, *Dogfight: True Stories of Dramatic Air Actions* (The History Press, 2009)

_____, *Focke-Wulf Fw 190 in Combat* (The History Press, 2009)

_____, *Spitfire: A Documentary History* (Macdonald and Jane's, 1977)

_____, *Spitfire: Pilots' Stories* (The History Press, 2012)

_____, *The Spitfire Story* (Silverdale, 2002)

Sakaida, Henry and Takai, Koji, *B-29 Hunters of the JAAF* (Osprey, 2001)

Sharp, Dan, *Luftwaffe: Secret Bombers of the Third Reich* (Mortons Media Group, 2016)

_____, *Secret Projects of the Luftwaffe: Blohm & Voss BV 155* (Tempest Books, 2019)

_____, *Spitfires Over Berlin* (Mortons Media Group, 2015)

Sommer, Erich, *Luftwaffe Eagle* (Grub Street, 2018)

Von Lunen, Alexander, *Under the Waves, Above the Clouds: A History of the Pressure Suit* (Darmstadt University of Technology, 2010)

Newspapers, magazines and journals

Aeroplane Monthly

Air Forces Magazine

Aviation News

Bristol Post

FlyPast

The Glasgow Herald

Journal of Aerospace Medicine
London Gazette
Military History Magazine
Sydney Morning Herald

Archives and official documents

Air Ministry Bulletin No. 12962
The Strategic Air Offensive Against Germany: 1939 – 1945 (HMSO, 1961)
United States Strategic Bombing Survey Report – Pacific War (National
    Archives and Records Administration, 1946)
National Archives (UK):
    AIR 20/6044 ('Sub-stratosphere flying: Future of Welkin aircraft')
    AIR 2/5583 ('Sub-stratosphere interception: policy')
    AIR 40/182 ('Junkers Ju 86P high-altitude aircraft')
    AIR 37/587 ('Allied Expeditionary Air Force: Welkin aircraft: policy')
    AIR 50/396 (Plt Off Galitzine's combat report, 12 September 1942)
    AIR 50/448/4 (Plt Off Genders' combat report, 6 September 1942)
    AVIA 18/716 ('Mosquito aircraft: performance and handling trials')
    CAB 79/60/47 ('High Altitude Bombers – Report by the Joint
        Intelligence Sub-Committee')
    CAB 80/28/1 ('Requirement of AA guns for dealing with high altitude
        targets')
    CAB 79/11/26 (Chiefs of Staff Committee meeting, 7 May 1941)
    CAB 65/27/35 (Cabinet meeting, 31 August 1942)
    CAB 195/1/36 (Cabinet meeting, 7 September 1942)
    HW 1/2078 (signal intercept, 1 October 1943)
    Operations Record Books (various squadrons)

Audio interviews

Ayerst, Peter (IWM tape: 30001)
Jones, Francis (IWM tape: 9397)
Lucas, Philip Gadesden (IWM tape: 12878)
Penrose, Harald (IWM tape: 17827)

TV documentaries

Fight Above the Clouds (Eureka Media, 2013)

Websites

www.airandspace.si.edu
www.andersen.af.mil
www.bbc.co.uk/history/ww2peopleswar
www.en.wikipedia.org.uk
www.ghostbombers.com
www.history.nasa.gov
www.junkers.de
www.nuremberg.law.harvard.edu
www.peoplesmosquito.org.uk

Index

Dear Reader,

We hope you have enjoyed this book, but why not share your views on social media? You can also follow our pages to see more about our other products: facebook.com/penandswordbooks or follow us on Twitter @penswordbooks

You can also view our products at www.pen-and-sword.co.uk (UK and ROW) or www.penandswordbooks.com (North America).

To keep up to date with our latest releases and online catalogues, please sign up to our newsletter at: www.pen-and-sword.co.uk/newsletter

If you would like a printed catalogue with our latest books, then please email: enquiries@pen-and-sword.co.uk or telephone: 01226 734555 (UK and ROW) or email: Uspen-and-sword@casematepublishers.com or telephone: (610) 853-9131 (North America).

We respect your privacy and we will only use personal information to send you information about our products.

Thank you!